1.95

LOIRE VALLEY

GU00715417

By the staff of Editions Berlitz

Preface

A new kind of travel guide for the jet age, Berlitz has packed all you need to know about the Loire Valley into this compact and colourful book, one of an extensive series on the world's top tourist areas.

Like our phrase books and dictionaries, this book fits your pocket—in both size and price. It also aims to fit your travel needs:

- It concentrates on your specific destination—the Loire Valley—not an entire country.

- It combines easy reading with fast facts; what to see and do, where to shop, what to eat.

- An authoritative A-to-Z "blueprint" fills the back of the book, giving clear-cut answers to all your questions, from "How much does it cost to rent a car?" to "Where can I find a baby-sitter for the evening?"—plus how to get there, when to go and what to budget for.

- Easy-to-read maps in full colour pinpoint sights you'll want to see.

In short, this handy guide will enhance your enjoyment of the Loire Valley. From the châteaux and their intriguing history to the tempting shops of Orléans, from the fascinating museum of Tours to the culinary delicacies which have made France famous, Berlitz tells you clearly and concisely what it's all about.

Let your travel agent help you choose a hotel.

Let a gourmet guide help you find a good place to eat. But to decide "What should we do today?" travel with Berlitz.

Photography: Claude Huber
Layout: Doris Haldemann
We're particularly grateful to Ewa Moberg for her help in the preparation of this book. We also wish to thank the French State Tourist Office.

Cartography: Falk-Verlag, Hamburg.

Contents

Maps: Loire Valley pp. 18–19, Orléans p. 21, Blois p. 23, Tours p. 29, Saumur p. 32, Angers p. 33.
Cover: Château de Saumur.

How to use this guide
If time is short, look for items to visit which are printed in bold type in this book, e.g. **Chaumont.** Those sights most highly recommended are not only given in bold type but also carry our traveller symbol, e.g. **Chambord.**

The Region and its People

"Soft and sensual"—that's how a famous 19th-century French historian described the Loire Valley, and that just about sums it up perfectly.

You'll remember those words when you stop along the Loire and watch its blue waters gliding lazily between tree-lined banks and around snug little islands. Or when you experience the bewitching quality of the light; at once crystalline and mellow, it's so subtle that very few painters have dared attempt to capture it on canvas.

A multitude of writers and poets from the Middle Ages to the present day have endlessly vaunted its peacefulness and sweetness of living. And if that still holds good in our own fast-living age, it's no wonder that so many kings, favourites, ministers and courtiers should have made this corner of France the most sumptuous residential area of all time.

With some 120 major châteaux in all, each more grandiose than the next, the Loire Valley can claim the highest concentration of them per square mile anywhere on earth. Strategy and aesthetics don't usually mix, but wherever a château may be—at the water's edge or in a shady valley, towering above a town or in a majestic forest—aesthetics win the day every time. You'd need a lifetime to explore them all in detail, but what you'll see, even on a short visit, will be something

The majestic Loire wends its way past charming towns and scores of châteaux; pondering purchase at the open-air market (left).

to remember for a lifetime.

Loire Valley people were created in its image. They're exactly like their landscape: gentle and even-tempered, friendly. You'll find them invariably helpful, seldom hurried. They're still country folk at heart, even in the towns.

Linguistic traditions in the Loire Valley are strong, and it's no coincidence that more writers and poets have been born there than, say, scientists. Among the most famous are François Rabelais, creator of Gargantua; Charles, the poet-Duke of Orléans who languished for 25 years in the Tower of London; du Bellay, Belleau and Ronsard, members of the immortal group of French 16th-century poets; the philosopher Descartes ("I think, therefore I am"); nearer our times, Vigny, Balzac, Courteline, Charles Péguy and Alain-Fournier, not to mention those who weren't born there but found inspiration to write under the Loire's skies.

The château country covers three distinct "provinces": the Sologne, Touraine and Anjou. If they differ in contour, they're similar in the mildness of their climate, their abundance of ponds and rivers and for that gentle quality of life that makes the Loire Valley.

Flat and wooded, the Sologne countryside has a pleasantly unkempt appearance. Its deep forests and silent clearings, its ponds and marshes are favourite haunts of huntsmen and fishermen. Flowers in profusion are grown here industrially. Orléans is famed for its rose nurseries and boasts a gigantic floral park. The Sologne is at its best in autumn with its radiant palette of gold and brown hues.

Touraine, aptly named "the garden of France", is predominantly agricultural. Its softly contoured, varied landscape, well-tended fields and neatly planted vineyards, the creamy whiteness of its stone and the natural elegance of its villages never fail to delight the eye.

Beyond Touraine, the Angevin landscape becomes more heavily etched, valleys grow deeper, hills more undulating. But the freshness remains. Anjou is all in blues and greens: from the blue of the Loire, of its sky and of its characteristic slate roofs, to the greenness of its orchards and its pastures. If the Touraine is France's garden, Anjou is its orchard, for it's a major fruit-growing region. Apple, cherry and plum blossoms give it a springtime bridal look.

And linking all three is the Loire itself, prima donna of Loire Valley rivers and, indeed, of all French rivers; it's the longest in France (628 miles), with its source in central France and its estuary at Saint-Nazaire (famous for the Second World War raid) on the Atlantic coast. Despite its languid appearance, seasonal fluctuations in level, dangerous currents and shifting sandbanks have gradually discouraged all forms of serious navigation, although barges laden with wine casks plied along it for centuries. The Loire now serves no purpose at all other than that of giving pleasure to the senses —and that's service enough.

Old-fashioned finery and antique car in colourful summer parade.

A Brief History

From its remotest past to our own day, the Loire Valley has had more than its fair share of wars and violence. It has seen the passing of kings, queens and courtiers, of saints, sinners, pirates, soldiers, poets and writers, royal mistresses often more famous than the kings whose beds they graced, larger-than-life characters good and bad, all part of a centuries-long pageant that has made French history.

For the Loire Valley has been "making" history longer than you'd probably care to remember. Its menhirs and dolmens bear mute witness to a prehistoric human presence; Gallic tribes flourished here; its Roman remains show a conqueror's appreciation for strategy and the unfailing aesthetic Roman eye for landscape, while Gallo-Roman treasure troves testify to its rapid prosperity.

St. Martin of Tours made it the cradle of French monasticism in the 4th century A.D.; Attila's Huns came within sight of it in the 5th; the Frankish kings prized it; 8th-century Moslem invaders from Spain nearly overran it; Charlemagne chose to make it the cultural centre of his mighty European empire. Scarcely literate himself, he founded a renowned multi-national Palace School at Tours. Directed by Abbott Alcuin, a Yorkshireman, it produced some of the finest medieval manuscripts in Europe.

By the 10th century, savage Norman raiders sailed up the Loire, spoiling for the rich plunder of prospering towns and abbeys. An equally savage Angevin count, Foulques Nerra, "the Black Falcon", followed in their footsteps, rampaging over the region, building strings of massive

defensive forts, many on Roman sites, and themselves the sites of future Loire châteaux.

England versus France

By a lucky marriage, a line of Angevin counts, the Plantagenets, were to rule England for over three centuries (1154–1485)—from Henry II to the notorious Richard III (the Princes-in-the-Tower murderer). English history owes the Plantagenets its

Statue of 4th-century St. Martin and prehistoric megalith near Doué speak of Loire's rich past.

most romanticized kings—Richard the Lion-Heart, John (of Magna Carta fame) and Henry V (victor of Agincourt).

The early Plantagenets spent more time in their beloved Anjou than in England; Henry II and his son Richard both died at Chinon and both lie buried at Fontevraud Abbey (see p. 32). English and French history in this period are inextricably mixed, and these Angevin kings of England left a lasting mark on the Loire Valley.

Fiercely fought over by Plantagenets and French, Anjou and Touraine were largely regained by the French in King John's reign, but nearly lost again to England in one of history's bitterest, longest struggles. English claims to the lands and Crown of France sparked off a series of wars and campaigns fought on French soil, better known as the Hundred Years' War (1337–1453).

French national heroine Joan of Arc's miraculous adventure began at Chinon in 1429, ending brutally at the

Many Plantagenet kings and their consorts lie buried in the impressive Abbey of Fontevraud.

stake scarcely two years later. But the flame that finally roused the French to something like national resistance couldn't be put out.

By the late 15th century, spiderish, autocratic Louis XI had brought much-needed peace and stability to the country, setting up, among other things, a thriving silk industry at Tours. Anjou itself had long since passed to France; Brittany, last of those menacing independent duchies, was about to fall into French royal hands by marriage. Henceforward, the Loire Valley was to come into its own as a place of pure pleasure. Uncomfortable feudal fortresses became unnecessary anachronisms. In France, as in contemporary Tudor England, château-building was soon to undergo a violent change.

Charles VIII and Louis XII returned from fruitless Italian military campaigns brimming with enthusiasm at what they'd seen and determined to "go Renaissance". Italian architects, decorators and landscape gardeners began to trickle in, but it was left to Francis I to deal the final deathblow to an all-French Gothic style of building. His was the age of Chambord, Azay-le-Rideau and Chenonceau.

Religious Strife

Spreading Protestant ideas in the early 1500s caused renewed strife in France. Saumur and Angers, prosperous trading towns, became powerful Protestant centres. For the next 80-odd years the country was caught in the throes of fratricidal, intermittent religious wars between Catholics and Huguenots (Protestants), culminating in the 1572 St. Bartholomew's Day massacre of Protestants in Paris.

Former Protestant Henry IV's Edict of Nantes (1598) attempted to grant the Huguenots freedom of worship. Less than a century later, in 1685, Louis XIV revoked the edict, outlawing them and causing masses to emigrate. Industrious Loire Valley artisans joined other Huguenots seeking the sanctuary of Protestant England, Holland and Switzerland. The Swiss watch industry probably owes a lot to skilled watchmakers from Blois who settled there.

During the Sun King's long reign (1643–1715), the royal scene shifted more or less permanently to Versailles. Royal visits to the Loire be- **13**

Francis I, as depicted by Clouet; right: arms in Blois window, Anne of Brittany's ermine and porcupine emblem of Louis XII.

André Held

came infrequent; some of its finest châteaux became state prisons; but a host of historic personalities still came, went or lingered here throughout the 18th century.

Since the Revolution

Miraculously, major châteaux survived the Revolution relatively intact, though many valuable furnishings were destroyed or auctioned **14** off, the buildings often ser-

ving as barracks or stables well into the 19th century.

The mid-19th century saw many châteaux pass into less aristocratic but more moneyed hands, as ambitious captains of industry bought and often restored them to something of their former glory. The 1870–71 Franco-Prussian War brought more violence. But this was insignificant next to the nightmarish devastation during the 1940 Nazi invasion of France. All main Loire towns from Gien and Orléans to Tours and Angers were mercilessly bombed, and irreplaceable old buildings destroyed. The Loire was at its shallowest that year; German tanks surged across, but the inhabitants of Saumur still proudly recall the heroic handful of unequipped cavalry school cadets who held off an entire Panzer division for two days.

Allied bombings caused further destruction before the liberation, but post-war reconstruction was rapid. Local industries revived. The scars have healed. Those seemingly unchanging landscapes are as serene as they've ever been, and the Loire itself flows on through it all, splendidly aloof, a majestic pacemaker of history.

A Who's Who to Loire Valley History

St. Martin of Tours
(316–97)

Soldier-turned-priest, "Apostle of the Gauls", founded numerous monasteries. Universally remembered as a symbol of charity for cutting up his cloak to share with a pauper. Died at Candes; buried at Tours.

Roi René
(1409–80)

Duke of Anjou and King of Sicily. Popular figure known to contemporaries as Good King René. Cultivated, literate, a fine linguist, his interests were limitless. A true Renaissance ruler, he made Saumur

and Angers cultural centres. Daughter Margaret married Henry VI of England.

Charles VII
(1403–61)
His name is forever linked to Chinon. There, as uncrowned King of France, he received Joan of Arc, who was to have him crowned at Reims almost despite himself. His reign saw the end of the Anglo-French Hundred Years' War.

Joan of Arc
(1412–31)
Humble peasant girl with a mission, she saved France from English domination, freeing town after town along the Loire, including Orléans, and winning battle after battle. Captured and tried, she was burnt at the stake at Rouen by the English and declared a saint in 1920.

Louis XI
(1423–83)
Son of Charles VII. Crafty, cruel and superstitious, yet a highly able ruler who reunified France by guile and diplomacy. Bitterest enemy of Charles the Bold of Burgundy. Built Langeais, often resided at Plessis-lès-Tours where he died. Buried at Cléry-Saint-André, near Orléans.

Charles VIII
(1470–98)
Son of Louis XI. Married Anne of Brittany in 1491, thereby adding independent Brittany to France. He rebuilt the château at Amboise and died there at the age of 28, due to an accident.

Anne of
Brittany
(1477–1514)
Associated especially with Langeais, Amboise, Loches, and Blois where she died. Married Charles VIII, then his successor Louis XII, keeping Brittany French. Her arms, the ermine and cords of St. Francis, are frequently to be seen.

Louis XII
(1462–1515)
Son of Charles, poet-Duke of Orléans. Born at Blois, lived there most of his life. His arms, the porcupine, are prominent at Blois and Amboise.

Francis I
(François Ier)
(1494–1547)
The Loire Valley's "star" king. Educated, charming, seductive, brave, fond of good living—and well over 6 feet tall! We owe him Chambord. Married Claude, daughter of Louis XII. His arms, the salamander, can be seen in many a Loire château.

Catherine
de' Medici
(1519–89)
Italian wife of Henry II of France, daughter-in-law of Francis I and mother of three French kings (Francis II, Charles IX, Henry III). An unscrupulous intriguer, she was personally involved in the St. Bartholomew's Day massacre of Protestants in Paris. Lived at Blois and Chenonceau, which she enlarged.

16

Where to Go

Whether based in Orléans, Blois or Amboise, Tours, Saumur or Angers, or anywhere near them, you'll find more than enough to fill your day with things to see and do, and keep the whole family happy. Each of these centres is a convenient hub from which to radiate either by car, bus, cycle or on foot and visit a series of châteaux (see map, pp. 18 and 19).

Time off from château-visiting to relax on a lazy riverbank with Chambord in the background.

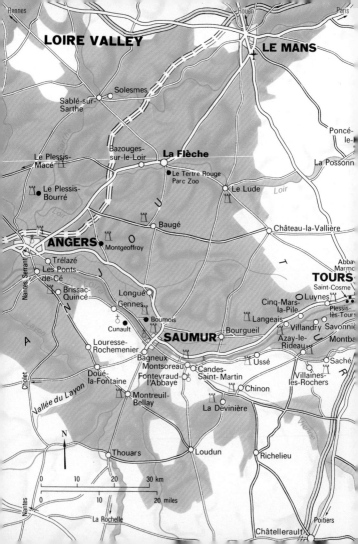

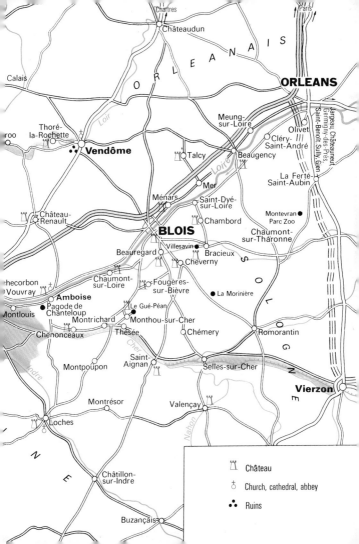

	Château
	Church, cathedral, abbey
	Ruins

ments, human characters and masses of natural and man-made curiosities (see p. 75). Don't hesitate to turn off now and then from those well-trodden pilgrim paths to the châteaux; your holiday will be all the more unforgettable for it.

The Towns

While the châteaux are the prima donnas of the Loire Valley, the region's main cities contain enough sights of interest to take up an entire holiday on their own. You'll find them fascinating to explore for their picturesque, historic streets and buildings, for their shopping, for their museums and curiosities, for their highly individual atmospheres. You'll experience the near-Parisian sophistication and attractiveness of Orléans; the cheerful cosiness of Blois; the pleasant, relaxed mood of Amboise; the grandness and quaintness of Tours; the old-world charm of airy Saumur; and that of Angers, so venerably historic yet so young in spirit.

Even if the châteaux are your principal objective, take time off to enjoy these unique towns. Your Loire Valley impressions won't be complete without them.

Some younger tourists found an alternative to walking tours.

From Orléans to Angers, we'll point out landmarks and places you shouldn't miss. But whether it's an ancient country church or a windmill, an unexpected panorama or a secluded pond, a forgotten hamlet or some village *bistrot*, you're bound to discover a great deal more if you have the time to explore for yourself.

For the Loire Valley is a heady cocktail of landscapes, **20** history, architectural monu-

Orléans

Pop. 100,000

A pleasant, airy, prosperous university city, it's so close to Paris by train that it could pass off as a suburban extension to the capital.

Joan of Arc (who relieved Orléans under English siege in 1429) is present everywhere here: there's the house she stayed in *(Maison de Jeanne d'Arc);* there are statues of her—one on horseback in the city's main Place du Martroi; a *rue* and a Lycée Jeanne d'Arc and lavish annual memorial celebrations *(Fêtes de Jeanne d'Arc)* early in May (see p. 78).

Orléans boasts a good number of churches, its most famous, Saint-Aignan, dating from the 15th century, but with an early 11th-century crypt. The city's awe-inspiring, Gothic-style Cathédrale Sainte-Croix was surprisingly completed between the 17th and 19th centuries, despite its 10th-century crypt. Don't miss some interesting, picturesque old buildings: the Maison de la Coquille, Maison d'Alibert (both on Place du Châtelet) and Maison de François Ier; the 16th-century City Hall *(Hôtel de Ville)* on Place de l'Etape; the early 16th-century building now an important **Fine Arts Museum** *(Musée des Beaux-Arts)* on Place de la République; the 18th-century Rue Royale, elegantly arcaded shopping street.

Outside Orléans

Hundreds of thousands of flower bulbs, plants, endless

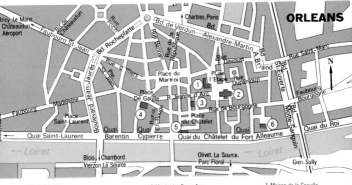

ORLEANS

1 Hôtel de Ville
2 Cathédrale Sainte-Croix
3 Musée des Beaux-Arts
4 Maison de Jeanne d'Arc
5 Maison de la Coquille
6 Eglise Saint-Aignan

varieties of trees and shrubs make Orléans' 90-acre **floral park** (*Parc Floral de la Source*) a riot of colour and a cool haven of rest. Spend an afternoon strolling in it, take a trip around it on a small electric train, see the source of the River Loiret as it bubbles up into a large circular pool.

Then visit nearby OLIVET, a smart residential suburb along the Loiret. Hire a rowing-boat and get a swan's eye view of attractive waterside bungalows or join courting couples and groups of students sipping aperitifs at one of its romantic riverside café-restaurants.

GIEN, 64 kilometres east of Orléans, famous for its château-museum of hunting and its exquisite chinaware (see pp. 74 and 79), is worth the detour. On the way, stop at CHÂTEAUNEUF-SUR-LOIRE (château and Museum of Loire Navigation); at GERMIGNY-DES-PRÉS visit the cosy little church with a remarkable masterpiece—an 8th-century Carolingian **mosaic,** the oldest in France; at SAINT-BENOÎT, see the impressive **Romanesque basilica** (10th to 13th century) of one of Europe's most historic Benedictine monasteries; and at SULLY-SUR-LOIRE you'll want to visit the massive, moated château (see p. 74).

On the road from Orléans

Among the treasures of superb St-Benoît, its exquisite capitals.

to Blois, take a look at
Meung-sur-Loire, **Beaugency** (see p. 73) and Cléry-
Saint-André. Louis XI, buried at Notre-Dame-de-Cléry,
frequently came here in his
lifetime to try out his future
tomb for size.

Exploring from Orléans

North: *Châteaudun (48 km.), Char-
tres (72 km.);* **East:** *Jargeau (18
km.), Châteauneuf-sur-Loire (25
km.), Germigny-des-Prés (29 km.),
Saint-Benoît (35 km.), Sully-sur-
Loire (45 km.), Gien (64 km.);*
South: *Olivet (5 km.), La Ferté-
Saint-Aubin (21 km.), Chaumont-
sur-Tharonne (50 km.);* **South-West:**
Cléry-Saint-André (15 km.); **West:**
*Meung (14 km.), Beaugency (20
km.), Talcy (40 km.)*

Blois

Pop. 45,000

Agreeably bustling, hilly, it's
the snuggest of Loire Valley
towns and, despite severe war
damage, retains an old-world
French provincial flavour.

Explore narrow, winding
streets like Pierre-de-Blois,
du Chant-des-Oiseaux, des
Papegaults, Place Saint-Louis
and their picturesque old
buildings. Window-shop in
Rue Porte Chartraine, Porte
Côté and along lively Rue
Denis Papin, named after the
17th-century steam pioneer.
See the statue of Papin,
Blois-born, perched above
theatrical steps. Visit 17th-

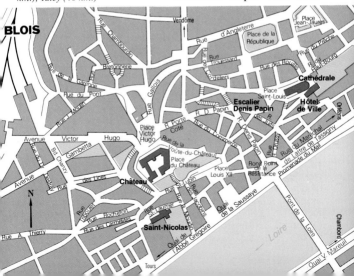

century Cathédrale Saint-Louis (10th-century crypt) and enjoy the view from the terrace of the bishop's palace nearby.

Quaint Rue Saint-Lubin will lead you up to the **château** (see p. 48).

Outside Blois
Besides its own château, Blois is excellently placed for some of the best-known ones like **Chambord, Cheverny, Chaumont** (see THE CHÂTEAUX IN DETAIL). But there are others, equally fascinating, just as accessible: BEAUREGARD, with its unique 17th-century portrait gallery (363 panelled portraits of great international historical characters) and a remarkable Delft-tiled floor giving an illusion of an army on the march; MÉNARS, Madame de Pompadour's château, with its splendid 18th-century kitchens and stately Loire-side gardens; graceful, Renaissance VILLESAVIN (built at the same time as Chambord) near BRACIEUX, a pretty village with a 16th-century wooden market-hall; FOUGÈRES-SUR-BIÈVRE, forbiddingly feudal; CHÂTEAU-RENAULT; LA POSSONNIÈRE, the poet Ronsard's birthplace; PONCÉ, TALCY and others; the region simply bristles with châteaux. Not all are open to the public, but most can be glimpsed from outside.

And thirty-two kilometres north-west of Blois, there's VENDÔME, with its medieval castle ruins, its **Abbatiale de la Trinité**—a Gothic gem—and picturesque Renaissance and 17th-century buildings. There's also a museum of 1776 Americana, for General Rochambeau, who commanded French forces in Yorktown, was born and died here. His descendants still live in the family château at nearby THORÉ-LA-ROCHETTE.

Exploring from Blois
North-East: *Ménars (8 km.), Talcy (29 km.);* East: *Villesavin (15 km.), Chambord (16 km.), Bracieux (23 km.);* South: *Beauregard (7 km.), Thésée (9 km.), Cheverny (13 km.), Fougères-sur-Bièvre (19 km.), La Morinière (29 km.), Chémery (36 km.);* West: *Chaumont (20 km.), Château-Renault (34 km.);* North-West: *Vendôme (32 km.), Thoré-la-Rochette (41 km.), La Possonnière (65 km.), Poncé-sur-le-Loir (72 km.), Le Mans (109 km.)*

Amboise
Pop. 10,000
Refreshingly peaceful, happy and relaxed, Amboise could be an excuse for a day or two's pause or a base to ex-

24

plore from. The town comes to life on its Sunday riverside market-day, but at the foot of its château there's year-round activity: souvenir shops, tea-rooms and antique shops cater to a stream of tourists. Strategically placed hotels, restaurants and some excellent local campsites afford fine views of the Loire.

On-the-spot sights include the **château,** the manor of **Clos-Lucé** (see p. 40) and the Postal Museum (*Musée de la Vieille Poste*).

Contrasts in Amboise: a modern fountain by Max Ernst; below: view of riverside from château.

Outside Amboise

Three kilometres to the south stands the solitary Pagode de Chanteloup, marooned in the grounds of a vanished 18th-century château built by Louis XV's minister Choiseul. There's a good panoramic view from the top. From Amboise you're within easy reach of **Chenonceau**— the most celebrated, most romantic château of them all, with its unique gallery-bridge over the River Cher (see p. 55). Be one of the 600,000 visitors who pass annually through its doors. Smoothly run on British stately home lines, it offers as tourist bonuses superbly tended gardens and canned 16th-century music.

Drive on up the Cher, through MONTRICHARD, to the château of GUÉ-PÉAN or to SAINT-AIGNAN and SELLES-SUR-CHER; then on to **Valençay** (see p. 69), MONTRÉSOR, **Loches** (see p. 65) and MONTPOUPON.

At Amboise itself and in some neighbouring localities (Montrichard, Montlouis, Vouvray), you'll find more picturesque wine-cellars-in-the-rock and tempting restaurants than you'll have time to see or eat in. Follow your instinct; you can't go wrong.

Exploring from Amboise

South-East: *Montrichard (23 km.), Monthou-sur-Cher (33 km.), Gué-Péan (34 km.), Saint-Aignan (40 km.), Selles-sur-Cher (54 km.), Valençay (68 km.);* **South:** *Pagode de Chanteloup (3 km.), Chenonceaux (13 km.), Loches (35 km.);* **West:** *Montlouis (13 km.), Vouvray (15 km.)*

Tours

Pop. 133,000

Capital of Touraine, already a "free" city in Roman times, now a major international congress centre, grand, rather dignified, business-like, it's also a university city with strong foreign and American student links. Pleasant, right-angled streets and broad tree-lined boulevards permit a constant fast flow of traffic, heavy except at night.

Tourists are well catered for with large numbers of hotels conveniently sign-posted at main-street intersections, a variety of restaurants, snack-bars, cinemas, nightspots, good shopping, theatre and còncerts and a convenient artificial lake for boating and swimming.

Among the city's several museums, don't miss the

Behind the modern trappings of Tours lies much medieval charm.

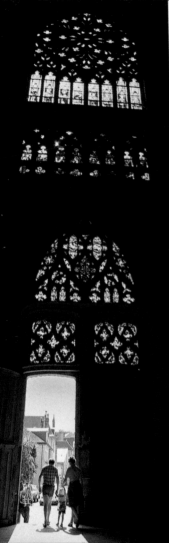

Musée des Beaux-Arts on the Place F. Sicard, whose outstanding collection includes Rembrandt and Mantegna paintings, and the unique Musée du Compagnonnage (national craft-guilds museum in the Rue Nationale).

Despite extensive Second World War bomb damage, parts of the **old town** still survive. You can see some fascinating medieval and Renaissance dwellings around the Place Plumereau, Place Foire-le-Roi and such streets as the Rue du Change, P.-L. Courier, Briçonnet, de la Scellerie and Colbert.

Religious buildings in profusion remind us that this was St. Martin's city, once a great centre of monastic learning. See the towering **Cathédrale Saint-Gatien** (13th-16th centuries), its superb 13th-century **stained glass** and pathetic tomb of Charles VIII and Anne of Brittany's children; visit the nearby Cloître de la Psalette; 13th-century Saint-Julien with its far older belfry, right in the bustling Rue Nationale; the curious Tour Charlemagne (Rue des Halles), said to have been

Thirteenth-century stained glass in the Cathédrale Saint-Gatien.

erected over the tomb of Queen Liutgarde who died here in 800; and the Renaissance Cloître Saint-Martin (Rue Descartes).

Outside Tours

A few kilometres in different directions from Tours are St. Martin's Abbey of Marmoutier with two unusual cave-chapels and the ruined Priory of Saint-Cosme where the poet Ronsard is buried (an impressive 12th-century refectory still survives).

Whether you decide on a locally organized day tour or go your own way, the choice is wide, and there are still more châteaux: the ruined keep at MONTBAZON, remains of a Foulques Nerra fortress; LUYNES, perched among its vineyards (no visits), with nearby remains of an impressive Roman aqueduct; derelict CINQ-MARS-LA-PILE, razed by Richelieu, with its own nearby Roman relic (the puzzling "Pile", or pylon); CHÂTEAU-LA-VALLIÈRE and **Le Lude** (see p. 74) to the north-west; then PLESSIS-LÈS-TOURS, **Villandry, Azay-le-Rideau, Langeais, Ussé** and **Chinon** to the west (see THE CHÂTEAUX IN DETAIL).

As a change from châteaux, sample two quiet

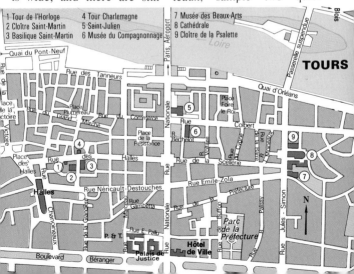

1 Tour de l'Horloge
2 Cloître Saint-Martin
3 Basilique Saint-Martin
4 Tour Charlemagne
5 Saint-Julien
6 Musée du Compagnonnage
7 Musée des Beaux-Arts
8 Cathédrale
9 Cloître de la Psalette

TOURS

Exploring from Tours

North: *Château-la-Vallière (33 km.), Le Lude (50 km.), Troo (55 km.);* **East:** *Abbaye de Marmoutier (3 km.), Rochecorbon (65 km.);* **South-East:** *Montrésor (58 km.);* **South:** *Villaines-les-Rochers (38 km.);* **South-West:** *Saché (28 km.), Azay-le-Rideau (28 km.), Chinon (49 km.), La Devinière (59 km.), Richelieu (61 km.);* **West:** *Saint-Cosme (4 km.), Plessis-lès-Tours (4 km.), Luynes (10 km.), Savonnières (13 km.), Villandry (15 km.), Cinq-Mars-la-Pile (18 km.), Langeais (23 km.), Bourgueil (42 km.), Ussé (43 km.)*

havens in timeless country settings: the manor house of SACHÉ, with its Balzac mementoes, where the novelist wrote some of his Loire-based books; and LA DEVINIÈRE, the birthplace of François Rabelais, the renowned 16th-century French writer.

The road along the Loire from Tours to Saumur, whether on the north or south bank, is one of the finest stretches in the Loire Valley. Restaurants, cafés, wine cellars, cool picnic spots and some picturesque "troglodyte" dwellings will tempt you to pause or linger.

Saumur

Pop. 25,000

A serene, roomy little town with predominantly white stone buildings and a strong 19th-century provincial flavour, it's the acknowledged equestrian capital of France, boasting a **national riding school** as famous as Vienna's.

The former Army School of Cavalry has long since converted to tanks, but the horse is still king here, and the best French and foreign military and civilian riders still come for instruction by the school's incomparable Cadre Noir (so-called for their characteristic black uniform). See their superb horsemanship in the great indoor riding school every Friday morning from October to June or the last week in July in their outdoor full-dress *carrousel* or tournament. The Tank School cadets also perform acrobatic feats on motorbikes. But for this you must book months ahead.

High above the town and Loire, the **château** (see p. 68), visible from everywhere, is at its best reflecting the early-morning light or at sunset.

The restored Romanesque **Church of Notre-Dame-de-Nantilly** is worth visiting for its fine collection of 15th- to 17th-century **tapestries.** You can reach it on foot from the château via pleasantly terraced Botanical Gardens.

Outside Saumur

From Saumur, the châteaux of BOUMOIS, MONTREUIL-BELLAY, MONTSOREAU and MONTGEOFFROY are within easy reach. And if you'd like further exciting, even off-beat suggestions for excursions on foot or by car, consult Saumur's dynamic tourist office.

Contrasting with Saumur's Protestant role in the 16th-century religious wars, three of the Loire Valley's most historic Catholic edifices, the

A horseman from Cadre Noir; below: the Loire at Saumur.

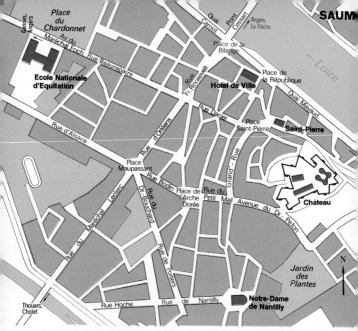

churches at **Candes** (12th–
15th century, concerts, superb panorama) and **Cunault**
(11th–13th century, Sunday
mass in Gregorian chant, 223
differently carved capitals)
and the great **Abbey of Fontevraud*** (12th–13th century,
Plantagenet tombs, refectory,
dormitory—a vivid impres-
sion of monastic life) are
visual experiences not to be
missed.

* Sometimes spelled Fontevrault, an
older form.

Exploring from Saumur

East: *Montsoreau (11 km.), Candes-
Saint-Martin (12 km.), Fontevraud-
l'Abbaye (15 km.);* **South:** *Bagneux
(1 km.);* **West:** *Doué-la-Fontaine (17
km.), Vallée du Layon (approx. 20
km.), Louresse-Rochemenier (23
km.);* **North-West:** *Saint-Hilaire-
Saint-Florent (3 km.), Boumois (6
km.), Cunault (11 km.), Gennes (15
km.), Montgeoffroy (31 km.)*

Angers
Pop. 135,000
Seen from its château's ramparts, Angers' slate roofs give
a deceptively sober impres-

sion; underneath it all, the place is alive and swinging. A university city, it caters generously for the young: trendy boutiques, discotheques, *pizzerias* and *crêperies* (pancake bars) abound.

Dress is casual, the atmosphere relaxed (the Loire Valley climate is at its year-round mildest here). You'll notice a Mediterranean flavour in Angers' public gardens. Take a stroll round the Jardin du Mail opposite the City Hall and around the Botanical Gardens.

After visiting the **château** (see p. 40), walk through narrow, quaint old streets and

up majestic steps to the **Cathédrale Saint-Maurice** (12th–13th century) with its beautifully coloured stained glass and rich treasure. Take a look at the 15th-century Maison d'Adam and its suggestive woodcarvings in the Place Sainte-Croix; see other picturesque dwellings in the Rue de l'Aiguillerie, de l'Oisellerie, des Poëliers and de Saint-Laud.

The 15th-century Logis Barrault (Fine Arts Museum) shows an impressive collection of 17th–18th-century paintings, engravings and sculptures, while the pleasing 16th-century Hôtel Pincé

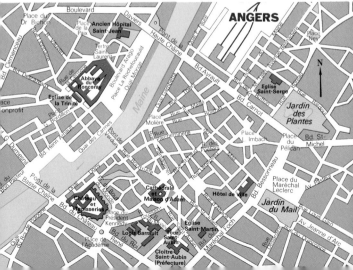

boasts some distinguished Far Eastern art.

And be sure to visit the 12th-century **Hôpital Saint-Jean.** Built by Henry II, it's the oldest hospital in France and probably in the world. The huge pillared sick-ward is a magnificent example of Plantagenet-style (otherwise

known as Angevin) vaulting. It now houses a series of symbolic modern tapestries by Jean Lurçat. Don't miss the chapel, loft and cellars, as well as the serenely peaceful cloister.

Angers is a religious city: its historic churches of **Saint-Serge,** Saint-Martin, de la Trinité and du Ronceray still fulfil their original purpose, drawing the faithful in impressive numbers.

Outside Angers

Around Angers, visit the great slate quarries at TRÉLAZÉ, LES PONTS-DE-CÉ, the châteaux of **Serrant, Brissac** and **Le Plessis-Bourré** (see pp. 73 and 74), LE PLESSIS-MACÉ, BAUGÉ (15th-century château and 17th-century Hôpital Saint-Joseph) and BAZOUGES.

Exploring from Angers

North: *Le Plessis-Bourré (19 km.), Baugé (38 km.), La Flèche (47 km.), Abbaye de Solesmes (59 km.), Le Mans (89 km.);* **East:** *Trélazé (8 km.);* **South-East:** *Le Plessis-Macé (14 km.), Brissac (16 km.);* **South:** *Les Ponts-de-Cé (6 km.);* **South-West:** *Cholet (70 km.);* **West:** *Serrant (17 km.)*

St. Maurice's pale belfries tower over Angers' black slate roofs.

The Châteaux in Detail

Château-visiting can make heavy demands on feet and mind. Unless really pressed, don't try to see too many in too short a time. You'll cherish the memory of five or six of them far more than you would an ill-digested dozen. And do not feel over-concerned about dates and architectural styles. Let the visual pleasure come before the history—drink in all the atmosphere, and your senses will do the rest.

For up-to-date information on opening times and entrance fees of châteaux and museums in the Loire Valley, you should obtain the handy brochure, "Val de Loire, pays des châteaux" from the French State Tourist Office in your country or from any tourist office on the spot. Issued annually, it contains, in addition, full details of Son et Lumière (sound and light) shows and lists major events of tourist interest.

Some Practical Information

The châteaux and museums charge entrance fees (see PLANNING YOUR BUDGET, p. 104), with reductions for children, **35** students and groups. Some offer half-price entrance on Sundays and holidays. Most of the châteaux are open year-round, including Sundays, but some are closed for a month or two in winter. In off-season, several close once a week, generally on Mondays or Tuesdays.

During the season (April to September) hours are generally from 9 a.m. to noon and 2 to 6.30 or 7 p.m. If you have a tight schedule of visits, do be sure to check opening and closing times in advance.

Only two of the châteaux, Chenonceau and Angers, offer on-the-spot eating and/or

refreshment facilities. But all provide first-class toilets and run postcard and colour-slide counters. Some of these also sell film, small souvenirs and coffee-table books on the Loire Valley.

At most châteaux you'll find attractive, spacious parks and gardens to stroll in at leisure once you've visited their interiors.

In season, sound and light (Son et Lumière) shows are presented at Azay-le-Rideau, Beaugency, Blois, Chambord, Chenonceau, Le Lude, Saint-Aignan-sur-Cher and Valençay.

The last three are floodlit, costumed pageants with a commentary. Blois alone presents an English version. *Promenades nocturnes* (night walks) around Azay and Chenonceau recreate the atmosphere of times gone by. For exact times and prices, consult local tourist offices (see p. 122–123).

On the following pages, the principal châteaux of the Loire Valley are presented in alphabetical order. Read the descriptions and make your selections.

Amboise and Clos-Lucé

Rebuilt and enlarged in the late 15th century by Charles VIII, who was born here, this formidable château, perched on its rocky pedestal high above the town, was conceived as a pleasure palace. Italian influence being as yet

Despite a forbidding, fortified appearance, château of Amboise began as a pleasure palace. 37

little felt, the overall impression is still that of a Gothic fortified place.

What you see of the castle today is a tiny portion of a once vast complex of buildings covering many times the present area, and even including a menagerie and early tennis court. Most of this was pulled down in Napoleonic times. A plan on the wall of the arcaded loggia overlooking the Loire shows the original extent in Charles VIII's time. There were huge Italian landscaped gardens, and some of the very first peach and orange trees to be planted in France were brought here by the king from Italy after his 1495 campaign. Some orange trees are still kept there.

Today's visitors enter the castle by a somewhat forbidding, narrow gateway. But if you'd been a guest of Charles VIII arriving by coach or on horseback, you would have reached the castle terrace in style via a broad spiral ramp within the **Tour des Minimes,** a 130-foot-high round tower with a superb if dizzying view from the top over the town's slate roofs and the Loire. Look down to the left at the castle edifice and you'll see a long balcony with a rusted iron balustrade. Known as the Plotters' Balcony *(Balcon des Conjurés)*, it served as a handy gallows in 1560 when savage mass executions followed an abortive Protestant plot to kidnap the young king Francis II. King and courtiers turned out to watch the hangings, jostling eagerly on this very tower, among them Francis' youthful wife, Mary, future Queen of Scots.

In the terrace gardens you'll see the 15th-century **Chapel of St. Hubert,** patron saint of huntsmen. Once hemmed in by buildings it stands alone today, an outstanding little gem of flamboyant Gothic architecture. Over its doors is a remarkable stone relief filled with detailed animals and trees, depicting St. Hubert's conversion. Above are stone kneeling figures of Charles VIII and his queen Anne of Brittany. As a final hunting touch, bronze antlers decorate the sides of the slender spire above the chapel. With an interior clearly designed for comfort, two stone fireplaces warmed the royal worshippers. According to tradition, and a memorial plaque dated 1592, Leonardo da Vinci is supposed to be buried beneath the chapel.

The **apartments** contain 15th- to 19th-century furniture, some 16th- and 17th-century Aubusson and Flemish tapestries, and several 19th-century Winterhalter portraits of the Orléans family, Napoleon III and the Empress Eugénie. There's also a magnificently carved 15th-century *trompe-l'œil* fireplace with cords threading in and out of the stonework. Symbols of the Franciscan Order, the cords were among Anne of Brittany's personal emblems, often seen with her familiar ermine arms. In the Louis XII wing, look out for the realistic pilgrims' staffs and purses carved in the stone window embrasures, a reminder that this part of the Loire Valley was a major staging post on the pilgrims' road to Santiago de Compostela.

Not a truly happy place, Amboise saw the accidental death of its builder, Charles VIII, who bumped his head violently against the lintel of a low door and died within hours. Under Louis XIV, the château became a state

The Clos-Lucé manor houses fascinating da Vinci exhibits.

prison. In the 19th century, it served briefly as a summer residence for King Louis-Philippe and, after his abdication in 1848, reverted once more to being a state prison; the 19th-century Algerian leader Abd-el-Kader was detained here. Present owner is the Count of Paris, a member of the Orléans family and a direct descendant of Louis-Philippe who was the last king of France.

Glance out of the windows as you walk through the rooms—the views are worth it. You'll be able to glimpse the manor of Clos-Lucé and, from the windows of the pillared Hall of the States General where Abd-el-Kader lived as a prisoner, you'll get a closer look at that Plotters' Balcony.

The manor of **Clos-Lucé** is only a short walk away from the château. Here Leonardo, painter of the *Mona Lisa* (called *La Joconde* by the French), artist and inventor of genius, lived out his last years, an honoured guest of Francis I. Tradition has it that the subterranean passage, whose entrance you can see, once linked the manor with the château, and that the king would often use it to visit the great man. The passage itself is blocked by fallen stones and remains unexplored.

Among exhibits relating to Leonardo and his work are a series of well-built, fascinating scale models of some of his inventions set next to his own sketches.

Some unexceptional frescoes in the little chapel have been attributed to one or more of his pupils, though it's said the ailing Leonardo just might have added a stroke here and there.

Leonardo died peacefully at Clos-Lucé in 1519—but not in the king's arms as they'd have us believe.

Angers

Most formidable of all the châteaux for its sheer size, Angers still fills modern visitors with awe.

Rebuilt on the site of a Gallo-Roman fortress by Foulques Nerra, 10th-century Count of Anjou, then held for a time by the Plantagenets, the castle as seen today dates from the first half of the 13th century. Louis IX (St. Louis) had it built as a defensive fortress in a record

Hallmark of Angers: layered construction of château's towers.

Angers' eloquent Apocalypse tapestry: superb medieval embroidery.

ten years, after which Anjou passed into the hands of the French Crown.

Its exterior appearance is made all the more forbidding by the locally quarried black slate used to build it. The architects themselves, no doubt, had qualms, for they tried to relieve the sombre blackness of the turrets with bands of white granite slabs imported from Brittany.

Seventeen in all, those mighty towers were once mightier still. During the 16th-century religious wars between Catholics and Protestants, the castle became too dangerous as a potential Protestant stronghold, and Henry III ordered it pulled down. Only the top floor-and-a-half of the turrets had been knocked down to rampart height when the king was murdered, and the castle was luckily reprieved.

One tower alone, the **Tour du Moulin,** survives at its original height, minus its pointed "pepper-pot" roof.

There's an all-round view from it of the Maine, the town and the cathedral. If you're afraid of heights, just climb to the first floor and take a stroll all around the castle along its 3,000-foot rampart promenade. From there you'll be able to admire the contrasting, graceful landscaped gardens, as well as the 15th-century chapel and the Royal Lodgings which both contain some fine tapestries. Tucked against the walls in its own little garden is a delightful 18th-century house, the Governor's Lodging. It houses a collection of 16th- and 17th-century French and Flemish tapestries.

If you didn't already spot them when you were entering the castle, look down into the ravine-like moat at the peaceful half-dozen deer who live in it. Not a tourist attraction, deer have been kept there since the mid-15th century when the amazing Roi René, Count of Anjou, filled the château grounds with exotic animals and ran a full-scale menagerie here, complete with lions. Doves are also still kept in the castle today.

Pride of Angers, however, is its world-famous, priceless

Apocalypse Tapestry. Dating from the late 14th century, it's held to be the oldest tapestry in existence and was commissioned for the castle by the then Count of Anjou, Louis I. It measured 550 feet in length by 16 feet in width. Seventy pieces of this remarkable work survive out of an original hundred, well displayed in a sober, modern, L-shaped building within the castle walls. A mere look at each scene would be enough

to appreciate the genius and skill of designer and weavers, but if you'd like a detailed 45-minute taped commentary in English, you can hire an audio device on the spot.

Incredible as it may seem, the tapestry was almost lost to us. Bequeathed to Angers' cathedral by Roi René, it was allowed to deteriorate through the centuries and was finally sold off in the 1840s as coverings for goods wagons! The Bishop of Angers bought it all back in the nick of time—for a song.

Azay-le-Rideau

Sixteenth-century Azay ranks among the Loire Valley's most famous and graceful châteaux. Built on a loop of the river Indre, one of the Loire's several affluents, it was erected, Venetian-style, on a foundation of wood piles close-driven into the mud.

Azay's history goes much further back in time, for a fortified castle already stood here in the 12th century, a feudal stronghold of the Ridel family from whom town and château take their name. (The local inhabitants are still referred to as Ridellois.)

The original castle was burned down and its 300-strong garrison slaughtered to a man in 1418 by the peevish Dauphin (the future Charles VII) in revenge for insults hurled at him as he marched by with his army on his way to shelter at Chinon. Known thereafter as Azay-le-Brûlé ("Azay the Burnt"), a ghost-ridden place of ill omen, it lay in ruins for exactly a hundred years.

Then came Gilles Berthelot, one of several royal ministers who were to build some

of the Loire's most sumptuous residences. Treasurer to Francis I, he married the heiress to the former Ridel lands and, during his spell in the financial saddle, set about building himself an elegant, comfortable retreat. Berthelot's wife, Philippe, personally oversaw the construction, and the château unmistakably betrays a feminine touch.

At first glance it might appear medieval, but those delicate turrets are of unmenacing proportions and clearly just meant to look decorative; windows and doorways carry tell-tale Renaissance pilasters and decorations, while the double-arched open loggias of the main staircase seen from the courtyard are certainly Italian in inspiration.

Reflections enhance the graceful proportions of Azay-le-Rideau.

Building went on from 1518 to 1527. With the second-floor interior still unfinished, Francis I cracked down and ordered an investigation of his minister's dealings, justifiably no doubt, since Berthelot promptly took to his heels. He died in exile and his dream-château duly passed into royal hands.

Inside, two points of notable interest are the **main staircase** and the kitchen. Until that time, stairs, usually steep and narrow, had always been built with an eye to easy defence in a spiral around a central pillar or round wall. A handful of men could hold off an army on them. You'll climb plenty of such stairs yourselves when visiting older châteaux.

Azay's staircase, built just like modern stairs, has straight lines with floor landings (the arcaded loggias) to mark the turns. It was, along with Chenonceau's, one of the very first to be so built in France.

The **kitchen,** a large vaulted room virtually at river-level, almost had running water, for here is an indoor well from which cooks and servants drew water straight from the Indre. The little niche in the wall next to it is no less than a sink. Below it is a stone drain for carrying used water back into the Indre. A practical woman's touch! Take a look also at the old iron cooking implements on the walls and the unusual wooden 17th-century cake moulds.

The apartments contain lavish ceiling and fireplace decorations, with the Berthelot's B and P monograms everywhere, as are the salamander and ermine arms of Francis I and his queen, put there by Berthelot as ostentatious compliments to his royal masters. A fine stone fireplace on the ground floor bears the only *crowned* salamander arms in the château. It was in fact put up after Francis I's confiscation of Azay, royal residences alone being entitled to such arms.

The furniture and tapestries are unworthy of this memorable château, but you'll find the views from its windows unforgettable. And before you go, take an outside look at Azay, admiring itself in its moat—a sight you'll long remember.

Italian influence is unmistakable in the spiral staircase at Blois.

⚜ Blois

The château at Blois is a unique marriage of three distinctive architectural styles.

Visitors enter by a gateway in the brick and stone wing built in traditional late Gothic style by Louis XII and completed early in the 16th century. Louis' equestrian statue over the gateway is a 19th-century replacement of the original. On the right-hand side of the gravelled courtyard stands the **Francis I wing,** the château's most famous part, with its striking Renaissance **staircase** and its outward-facing loggias, built by Louis XII's successor between 1515 and 1524. Immediately facing you across the courtyard, and in violent contrast to both, is the early 17th-century classical stone wing built from Mansart's designs for Gaston d'Orléans, brother of Louis XIII. The staircased main hall of this building is surmounted by an amazing elliptical dome high above a cut-away cupola. The overall interior effect is fantastic. As a sobering thought, all the stone-carving you can see was carried out on the spot by artisans working on scaffolding.

Strategically perched well above the town, the château was almost certainly built on the site of a Roman fort. The oldest surviving parts of it are the 13th-century Tour du Foix on the terrace and part of the outer wall of the great Hall of the States General tucked away between the Francis I and Louis XII wings. From the open terrace by the Tour du Foix you'll have a fine view over Blois and the Loire.

The château, now municipally owned, is very much a part of the town's life; Mansart's wing houses an important public library. Private wedding receptions are also held here. The Louis XII wing contains a museum of sacred art and an excellent fine-arts museum, intelligently displaying paintings, objects and furniture of similar period. You can visit both at leisure once you've been over the historic apartments in the Francis I wing.

You'll find a host of royal arms and monograms, reminders of a passing procession of kings, queens and of a succession of events that made French history. From Anne of Brittany and Claude de France's ermines, Louis XII's porcupine and Francis I's salamander to Louise de Savoie's arrow-pierced swan and Henry IV's H, they're carved on staircases, gateways and doors, on ceilings or over massive painted and gilded stone fireplaces.

Here, in 1440, the gentle poet-Duke Charles of Orléans, captured at Agincourt, came home after 25 years' captivity in London's grim Tower. He lived serenely at Blois surrounded by artists and writers, and the roguish poet Villon stayed with him for a time. Anne of Brittany, twice queen of France as wife of Charles VIII and Louis XII, loved the place and died here in 1514. Louis XII, son of Charles of Orléans, was born and lived here for a great deal of his life. Francis I found it a congenial residence and handy for its choice of nearby forests to hunt in—even after he'd built Chambord. His daughter-in-law, Catherine de' Medici, found it more secure than plot-ridden Paris, as did her three royal sons.

Catherine made herself at home here, and you'll see on the first floor of the Francis I wing the room she died in, her private chapel with its incongruous Gothic windows and her famous wood-panelled cabinet or study which survives exactly as she knew

it. Dating from about 1530, no two of its 237 carved and gilt panels are the same. The four "secret" cupboards, opened by a lever set at floor-level in the plinth, are thought to have been hiding places for some of those sinister Medici poisons, but no one really knows, even if

The art collection at Chambord is one of its main attractions.

Catherine herself did dabble in black magic.

Her daughter-in-law, Mary Stuart, ex-queen of France after the premature death of her husband Francis II, walked here with the poet Ronsard (who later escorted her back to her native Scotland to live out her tragic destiny). There's an attractive little portrait of her in the Fine Arts Museum.

On the second floor of the apartments you'll follow the steps of Henry, Duke of Guise, as he ran from the Council Chamber, desperately fighting to ward off his assassins' blades, collapsing finally in the king's bedroom. Two graphic 19th-century paintings on the walls recreate the scene.

Murdered on Henry III's

Chambord's maze of 365 chimneys form a surrealistic stage-set.

orders in 1588 (his brother, the Cardinal de Lorraine was similarly dispatched the next day), he had led the ambitious Guise clan's attempt to take control of the throne. 6½ feet tall, he was formidable in every way. A notorious ladies' man, the deep scar on his left cheek was said to have been inflicted by one of his many mistresses. It earned him the nickname Le Balafré ("Scarface"), but you'll never see it on any of his portraits, nor even on the posthumous one in the château, for he always had himself painted in half-profile.

In the 17th century, Marie de' Medici, mother of Louis XIII, confined here in disgrace, made a dramatic rope-ladder escape aided by the Cardinal Richelieu, and regained her lost influence over the throne. By the end of the 18th century, the château, uninhabited for years had been converted into a military barracks and was to suffer the consequences. In the mid-19th, the restorers took over and set to work to make the more historic parts live again, with unfortunate results. Sparsely furnished, the rooms are gloomily oppressive and the wall and floor decorations unpleasantly garish. It needs an effort of imagination to evoke the events that took place within them.

Chambord

Marvel of human achievement, an architectural extravaganza, a royal folly—whatever it is, Chambord can still make today's visitors gasp when they first set eyes on it.

The château sits in the middle of a 14,000-acre walled forest—the **Parc de Chambord,** a national game reserve patrolled daily by mounted members of the Garde Républicaine permanently billetted in the château. Wild boar, stags, deer and every variety of small game roam free in it. French presidential shoots are often held here for visiting heads of state and VIPs. Motorised visitors' movements are strictly regulated, and you should keep to sign-posted parking, viewpoint and picnic areas.

The park may give you a clue as to why Chambord was built. In the early 1500s, there was probably more game than there were trees. The counts of Blois were already hunting here 600 years before Francis I decided to build himself the largest hunting lodge in history.

For all its 440 rooms, this fairy-tale structure was to be little more than a mammoth pied-à-terre for a king and a suite of some 2,000 people, all intent upon the noble sport.

Work began in 1519, with the building more or less completed by the time of Francis' death 28 years later. Built of local Bourré stone like the later Cheverny, its dazzling white and "new" appearance is due to the quality of the stone which is said to grow harder and whiter with age.

No one knows for sure who designed it all. Italians certainly had a hand in it, to judge by the maze of fantastically ornate Renaissance chimneys (365 of them!) and lanterns on this **rooftop terrace.** Slate insets in the stonework imitating marble give an added Italian flavour. You can wander at will round this surrealistic stage-set-in-the-sky and gaze out over the forest of Chambord as far as the eye can see. And you'll be imitating the ladies of Francis' court, for this was their grandstand, conceived so they could follow every phase of the royal hunts. Catherine de' Medici preferred star-gazing to hunting and kept a permanent telescope up there.

Though hardly built in medieval fortress style, Chambord still retains traditional round turrets and originally even had a moat. This was covered over in the 18th century, probably on account of the mosquitoes that bred there, by the ex-King of Poland, Stanislas Leszczyński, Louis XV's father-in-law, who lived here for some time. Beyond Francis I, whose salamander arms appear all over it, the French kings cared little for the place. Never a comfortable residence, its rooms were too huge, it was and still is virtually impossible to heat adequately and was clearly too expensive to run. Louis XIV did come here on one of his rare visits to the Loire to see the première of Molière's now immortal *Le Bourgeois Gentilhomme,* with music specially written for the occasion by Lully.

After Stanislas' departure, Louis XV cast around elsewhere and gave it to Maurice de Saxe as a reward for beating the British at Fontenoy. The château successfully survived the Revolution, and

Napoleon continued royal buck-passing tradition, bestowing the place upon one of his more deserving generals.

Chambord's prime interior attraction is its monumental double-spiralled **grand staircase** which you literally "board" at each floor. There's a good chance that Leonardo da Vinci himself designed it before his death in 1519. It's certainly unique and unusual enough, for two people can step up or down it simultaneously and never meet! Try it for yourself and you'll be convinced.

The château momentarily came back to life in 1873 when the Count of Chambord, who'd been offered the French Crown, was all set to start out from there for Paris. At the last minute he refused because no one wanted to change the tricolor for the old Bourbon white flag of France. Those rather dusty, forlorn coaches, those liveries and harnesses under glass were all intended for his state drive through the capital. They've never been used.

Chaumont
Despite its splendid setting overlooking the Loire, Chaumont has seen a succession of illustrious residents come and go, few of them lingering long. Here, too, women have been closely involved in its history.

Rebuilt in the late 15th century by the Cardinal d'Amboise, Louis XII's minister, the château was later bought from his family by Catherine de' Medici. The crafty queen found a use for it when, on her husband's death, she "offered" it to his mistress, Diane de Poitiers, in exchange for cosier, more intimate Chenonceau which she'd long coveted.

A reluctant resident at Chaumont, Diane soon left it for the manor-house-château of Anet, outside of Paris, where she spent the rest of her life. In the 1800s, influential authoress-baroness Madame de Staël—banished from Paris by Napoleon due to her opposition to all political regimes in France—was an equally reluctant resident in Chaumont, missing even the Paris gutters!

Perhaps the outward reminders of a feudal castle, the massive pointed round towers, the drawbridge, proved too overpowering for feminine tastes. The château was indeed originally a medieval defensive fortress. Rebuilt in its present state around 1465, it was completed by 1510. More windows were later added, and one side of the main inner court pulled down to leave an open view over the Loire.

Chaumont, where Catherine de' Medici's astrologer foretold the violent death of her three sons.

Inside you'll see the bedrooms of the two rivals, Diane and Catherine, as well as that of Ruggieri, Catherine's evil genius, part-secretary, part-astrologer, part-poisoner.

There's a notable 17th-century Italian tiled floor; and an interesting collection

of terracotta portrait medallions of 18th-century personalities (including Benjamin Franklin) commissioned from an Italian artist, J.B. Nini, by Chaumont's owner, Jacques Le Ray who entertained Franklin in Paris and was to supply George Washington's army in 1776.

Don't miss the impressive stables, added in 1877, and enjoy a refreshing stroll in the château's inviting tree-shaded park.

✲ Chenonceau

Number one château for tourists, Chenonceau* is certainly unique in appearance.

Though no longer lived in, it's run on English stately home lines but goes one better, producing its own château-bottled wine for sale on the spot. You can ride a small electric train along the 500 yards from gates to château; hire a rowing-boat and glide in and out of the château's arches; have your children let off steam in a supervised free playground (open July–August); see 15 tableaux of Chenonceau's history in the little waxworks museum; eat

in an amusingly converted stable-restaurant, served by costumed "wenches"; or just stroll through 150 acres of green parkland. No regimented visits here; inside and out, you're free to wander at will.

The château's size will surprise and probably delight you. With just ten agreeably proportioned rooms, it's more like a snug manor-house. (The free-standing donjon/souvenir shop is an earlier 15th-century building.) The rooms on both floors open onto a hallway instead of one into the other —an innovation from privacy-conscious Renaissance Italy. The straight, Italian-style staircase was also one of the earliest seen in the region.

Built for his wife from 1513 to 1524 upon the arch of an old millhouse on the River Cher by royal financier Thomas Bohier, the château was surrendered to Francis I by Bohier's son to repay some of his father's "borrowings" from royal funds.

Diane de Poitiers, first and most famous of a long line of women owners (six of them in all), received it from her lover Henry II in 1547. Celebrated for her beauty and intelligence, she probably **55**

---

* Chenonceau or Chenonceaux? Traditionally, the village is written with an *x* — the château without.

owed her legendary health and complexion to regular washing and sensible eating—a rarity in those days—and is said to have swum often nude in the Cher. She had Chenonceau's gardens laid out, grew artichokes and had the famous bridge built on from the original manor (minus the covered gallery) to reach the opposite bank, crossing it to hunt—and to raise silkworms.

In the **apartments** you'll see the neat household accounts she kept, as well as some exceptional 16th-century Flemish tapestries; French, Italian and Spanish furniture; some good paintings, notably a Rubens, and a 16th-century portrait of her by Primaticcio as Diana goddess of hunting. The evocative kitchens, almost at water-level, are as she might have known them. There's one charmingly uncommercial touch in each room—a year-round bouquet of fresh flowers whose scent gives a lived-in feeling to the place. It would come as no surprise to see Diane herself laid on to welcome us!

She must have been too happy here, for on Henry's death his jealous widow, Catherine de' Medici im-

mediately packed her off to less congenial Chaumont and proceeded to erase all memory of her rival from the place. You'll see Catherine's  monogram spitefully plastered everywhere.

What was big enough for Diane was hardly big enough for Catherine. Picking up architect Philibert Delorme's original plans for the bridge, she had him cover it with two galleried floors, each 65 yards long, to serve as ballrooms and reception halls. Their cool, stone interiors reflect the simple, haughty grandeur of some Florentine *palazzo*. Yet how different is Cathe-rine's sumptuous little library with its lavishly carved wooden ceiling and its idyllic view over the Cher.

At stake in the rivalry between Diane de Poitiers and Catherine de' Medici: Chenonceau château.

France's teenage monarchs Francis II and Mary Stuart adjourned here with their court in 1560, fresh from the spectacle of those mass executions at Amboise (see p. 38) for a gay and extravagant celebration under Catherine's queen-motherly eye. Chenonceau was to see many more such festivities in her lifetime.

But after her son Henry III's murder in 1589, and her own death soon after, Henry's wife Louise of Lorraine retired here in widow's weeds, transforming the château into an extended funeral chapel. Some of her morbid decorations survive today. She even created a mini-convent of nuns in the loft above the galleries.

That same loft housed Jean-Jacques Rousseau in the 18th century. Voltaire was also a frequent visitor. The 19th-century owner, an ambitious lady, went bankrupt trying to restore Chenonceau to its former glory.

During the 1914–18 war, the Menier family, who still own it, turned Chenonceau into a military hospital, the galleries serving as wards and Diane de Poitiers' bedroom, of all things, as an operating theatre.

Cheverny

Built of stone quarried from nearby Bourré, Cheverny's exterior presents a dazzling picture of harmony and classical purity in its green parkland setting—a real delight to the eye. The interior, in contrast with the sober late Renaissance grand staircase, is all gilt and ornamentation, but its proportions are always human and of all the major châteaux, Cheverny is the one in which most visitors would like to live.

Owned by the Marquis de Vibraye, who resides in one of the château's wings, Cheverny has been lived in by members of the same family more or less uninterruptedly since the early 1600s when construction began.

Local architects, artists and craftsmen were closely involved in this all-French effort of building and decoration. Most of the painted ceilings and wall panels are the work of Blois-born Jean Monier, a successful 17th-century artist who spent 18 out of his 56 years of life painting at Cheverny alone. The panels in the King's Bedroom, and especially the Don Quixote sequence in the dining room, reveal a rare visual narrative talent.

There are some excellent **tapestries,** including a set of unique 17th-century Flemish country subjects after David Teniers, and some distinguished 17th and 18th-century furniture. One of the château's proudest possessions is a very fine 18th-century grandfather clock by Caffieri that tells not the hours but the days.

The grandiose **King's Bedroom** is full of Louis XIV atmosphere, though the Sun King never set foot in it. Since the Middle Ages, it was common practice in Europe for kings and their courts to move about the country from one royal estate to another. Noblemen's castles served as overnight halts in these royal progresses. Every château kept a room in constant readiness for the king, whether he ever passed there or not.

From the Salle des Gardes (guards' room), look out at the stately gardens and at the *orangerie* beyond. This typical lowbuilt, 18th-century greenhouse has one unique distinction: when the Louvre paintings were smuggled out of Paris during the Second World War, it sheltered the *Mona Lisa* (*La Joconde* in French) for six months under the very noses of German troops billeted in the château.

Cheverny takes great pride in its 70-strong hunting pack of hounds and is recognized as a mecca for devotees of the noble sport. Hunting (*chasse*) is here referred to by its grander name, *vénerie*. In the grounds you can visit the kennels and pat the dogs through the bars. Nearby is the Musée de Vénerie, a huge trophy room literally covered from floor to ceiling with some 2,000 stag antlers collected by the Cheverny hunt since 1850.

The Cheverny hunt meets twice a week from mid-October to mid-April. For tourists' benefit, in summer (two Saturdays in August) there's a floodlit description of a hunt complete with horn calls, hounds and a (dummy) dead stag. In July and August, two torch-lit hunting ceremonies held in the grounds attract several thousand visitors. If you have the chance, don't miss hearing those stirring French hunting horns.

Chinon

Although virtually all its buildings are in ruins, the château's 440-yard-long **ramparts** viewed from the oppo- **59** site bank of the Vienne leave you with an illusion of completeness.

Perched on a high rocky crag, it stands where a Roman fort formerly stood. You can still see remains of a Roman wall in the Château du Milieu (middle castle), so-called because Chinon is really three castles in one: Fort Saint-Georges, the Château du Milieu and the Château du Coudray, each with its own distinct access.

The counts of Blois and Anjou built most of it during the 10th century. By the 12th, it had passed into Plantagenet hands and was secure and comfortable enough to serve as a well-nigh permanent home for King Henry II of England. Fort Saint-Georges dates from his time. You'll see what little is left of it before crossing the stone bridge into the walled part of the castle. It was here, in the now derelict Royal Lodgings in the Château du Milieu, that this splenetic monarch died of rage in 1189 on learning that his sons Richard (the Lion-Heart) and John had turned against him. So unloved was he that his servants are said to have run off with everything they **60** could lay their hands on, stripping even the clothes off his corpse.

By 1205, after a year-long siege, the French wrested the castle from King John's grasp. In 1307, several leading Knights Templar were imprisoned here, awaiting the trial that led to their deaths at the stake in Paris and to the suppression of their order. You can still see some of their curious, near-cabalistic graffiti in the Donjon du Coudray, an impregnable round keep within the Château du Coudray. You must cross a moat to reach it from the Château du Milieu.

While in that part of the castle, don't miss a spectacular **view** over the town and the Vienne from the Tour de Boissy. To your right you'll see the castle's original keep, the 12th-century Tour du Moulin. All these towers were once topped with pointed tiled roofs that have long since disappeared.

In 1418, with the Hundred Years' War well underway and nearly all of France north of the Loire in English hands, the Dauphin (future Charles

Built to guard the Vienne, the forbidding walls of Chinon today still command imposing vistas.

VII) was hounded out of Paris by the English. Chinon offered the safety he sought, and here he stayed until a teenage country girl arrived one night 11 years later to change the course of French history. Chinon is above all "her" castle. Yet ironically enough, all you can see of the Great Hall in the Château du Milieu where Joan of Arc recognized the Dauphin hiding slyly among his 300 courtiers is a fragment of side wall with the remains of a large stone fireplace.

Visitors enter the castle by a curiously flattened **Tour de l'Horloge** (clocktower) which now houses a small Joan of Arc museum. At the top hangs a rather special bell known as Marie-Javelle. Cast in 1399, its peals have echoed regularly over Chinon for nearly 600 years. Joan herself would have heard it.

Chinon is just the place for lovers of mysterious underground passages. There are regular warrens within the castle walls (below the Donjon du Coudray, for one), not to mention the labyrinthine complex of "caves" at townlevel that burrow into the rock below the castle. Originally quarries from which the characteristic white *tuffeau*

(tufa) stone was extracted by the castle's medieval builders, they now serve mainly as wine cellars.

The last major historic event here was the arrival in great pomp of Cesare Borgia in 1498. He brought his father the pope's dispensation for Louis XII to divorce his wife and to marry his predecessor's widow, the all-important Anne of Brittany.

Cardinal Richelieu acquired the château in the 17th century, and he and his descendants completely neglected it for 200 years, allowing it to fall into its present ruined state.

In the town of Chinon, stroll through one of the most historic streets in the Loire Valley—the **Rue Voltaire,** with its high gabled stone or timbered houses. Richard I died in one of them; Joan of Arc dismounted there on arrival in the town. A medieval-costumed street-fair held each July brings it all to life. Don't forget to try Chinon's famous echo, at the foot of the north side of the château's ramparts.

Richard the Lion-Heart might have recognized Langeais.

Langeais

Langeais has everything a medieval fortified castle should have, from a massive drawbridge and portcullis to arrow-slitted battlements and covered catwalks with machicolations from which the defenders could pour boiling oil upon attackers rash enough to try to scale the walls with ladders.

This awesome, faintly sinister structure built in uncharacteristic grey stone dominates the little town of Langeais and commands an all-round view of the Loire and the countryside for miles.

The buildings you see date

only from the 15th century. Within the castle walls, and on an even higher mound, stand the tree-grown remains of a square keep. Put up by the prolific Foulques Nerra in 994, it's almost certainly one of the very first stone rectangular keeps ever built. (Until then they'd been made of logs.)

Langeais subsequently belonged to the Plantagenets until 1206 and was certainly familiar to Richard the Lion-Heart. During the Hundred Years War (1337–1453), the English captured it several times and only abandoned it finally in 1428 for a 2,000-crown ransom, on condition that the whole castle, except the keep, be pulled down.

Langeais stands at the crossroads of Anjou and Touraine, hence its strategic importance. When Louis XI decided to rebuild the castle, his motives were strictly defensive, for the powerful, ambitious dukes of nearby independent Brittany offered a constant threat to his throne. Though he didn't live to see it, he worked hard to bring about the marriage of his son Charles VIII to Anne, heiress to the Duchy of Brittany. The historic marriage took place in 1491 in one of the châ-

teau's rooms. Langeais became thereafter a mere residence to be bestowed on deserving subjects.

Most of its rooms, smaller than those in other châteaux, are agreeably human in proportion. The furniture (some of it reproduction), tapestries, and tiled floors repeating genuine 15th-century motifs are among the best you'll see in any Loire château. Everything here was painstakingly collected by a 19th-century owner, Jacques Siegfried, whose wealth, will and scholarship brought Langeais back to life. The rooms are hard to beat for real period atmosphere and give a good idea of what it was like to live in a castle in the late Middle Ages.

Among the many fine 15th- and 16th-century tapestries, have a close look at a vivid 15th-century hunting sequence on the ground floor. It's strikingly realistic, if bloodthirsty.

In the Salle des Gardes (guards' room) you'll see a curious 15th-century stone fireplace imitating castle battlements with crenellations and soldiers' heads looking down at you from them. And there are still more curiosities in store for you—Anne of

Agnès Sorel served as a model for Madonna in Fouquet work.

There's no risk, but watch where you step, for the machicolations along the edge are only covered with planking. The view from on top is worthwhile, so be sure to bring your camera.

Loches

Loches's castle sits upon a broad spur above the River Indre, the town's quaint houses appearing to huddle around it for protection.

Surrounded by over a mile of **fortifications** (there's a signposted walk round their exterior), it's a formidable place, even by modern standards. Almost a town in itself, it embraces a palace, a church, prisons and numerous picturesque old stone dwellings, most of which are still lived-in.

A castle has stood here since the 6th century. Fortified, then lost, by Henry II Plantagenet in the 12th, recaptured by his son Richard the Lion-Heart in a continuing struggle with the French kings, the coveted fortress fell finally to the French after a year-long siege in 1205. Joan of Arc stopped here in 1429 with her reluctant Dauphin on the way to Reims. Kings, queens and royal mistresses dallied here, though all too

Brittany's marriage chest, for one.

You'll have an unforgettable experience walking along the covered battlements or *chemin de ronde,* 25 yards above the town's rooftops.

soon and for far too long the place served as a state prison.

The massive **Porte Royale** is the castle's sole entrance. Its gatehouse, now a small regional museum *(Musée du Terroir)* reconstructs a farm kitchen scene complete with an elderly wax couple in local costume by the fireside. Don't miss a good view over the town from the top of the gatehouse. Nearby is the Lansyer Museum (19th-century Touraine landscapes, Ca-

Little has changed within the walls of Loches for 800 years.

naletto and Piranesi engravings, Far Eastern art).

To the right and on higher ground lies the oldest surviving part of the castle, a square 11th-century **keep** built by Foulques Nerra's grandson. With a height of 120 feet, it's a classic example of Romanesque military architecture. This, with a later 15th-century keep, and the notorious Martelet tower where prisoners were tortured or locked up, is tucked away at the southern end of the walls.

Within this sinister complex you'll be shown 15th-century torture instruments and hear all about Louis XI's special cages in which "choice" prisoners languished sometimes for years on end, suspended from the ceiling. You'll see the dark, comfortless cell where for eight years Duke Sforza of Milan was kept confined by Louis XII and the pathetic attempts he made to brighten it by painting those childlike decorations all over its walls. He's said to have died the day of his release, blinded by glare from the snow outside.

In total contrast to this historic misery, and at the castle's opposite end, are the almost lighthearted **Royal Lodgings** (Logis royal),

largely built under Charles VIII and Louis XII, and still very Gothic and very French in style. You'll see here a little gem of Gothic art: Anne of Brittany's private oratory. Elaborately niched, its stone walls are superbly carved with her ermine-tail arms and the symbolic cords of the Franciscan order.

In the Royal Lodgings, but originally in nearby Saint-Ours church, lie the remains and lifelike alabaster effigy of Agnès Sorel, mistress of Charles VII, Joan of Arc's Dauphin. Note the two lambs at her feet—a gentle pun on her name (agneau, lamb).

Eleventh- to 15th-century **Saint-Ours church** presents some amazing and unique Romanesque features. Carved over its main doorway is a medieval foretaste of hell—a nightmarish array of grimacing monsters and beastly deformities that sends a genuine shiver up the spine. Inside, look at the roof of the nave. It's made up of two peculiar hollow pyramids. From outside they appear as two towerless spires squatting where a roof should be.

Take your time looking around this fascinating, history-laden place. You'll find plenty more to intrigue you. **67**

Saumur

A Roman fortress almost certainly stood on the site of Saumur's castle, perched aloft on a hill. The castle's own origins go back to the 10th century, but the existing structure dates from the 14th and 15th centuries when it became a residence of the counts of Anjou, as they were then. The famous Roi René made it for a while a brilliant cultural centre for artists, musicians and scholars.

There's a hand-painted miniature of the château in the world-famous early-15th-century *Book of Hours* of the Duke of Berry. Its pointed turrets, gilt weather vanes and elaborate chimney stacks gave it a truly fairy-tale appearance which it has long since lost. And no wonder, for it became successively a defensive Huguenot fortress in the 16th century, a state prison in the 18th (the Marquis de Sade was locked up here) and an army barracks in the 19th. But it's still recognizable and still impressive.

Before visiting the interior, take in the view over the Loire and Saumur's blue-grey slate roofs from the courtyard terrace. For an even better all-round **view,** climb to the top of the **Tour de Guet** (watchtower), but mind the steep, spiral stairs. Then go below ground for a look at a terrifying little circular prison cell, definitely not meant for claustrophobics!

The well-like opening in the courtyard's centre is the ventilation shaft of a vast barrel-vaulted stone chamber below—the château's water reservoir. The small roofed building by the terrace parapet contains another shaft with an elaborate wooden winch which served to haul up food and ammunition brought directly from barges moored on the Loire, not far below the walls.

68

Robert Harding Associates

In the apartments, you can see an important and comprehensive collection of 17th- and 18th-century **French and Dutch china,** well worth lingering over if only guides weren't such hustlers.

The château's pride is its **Equestrian Museum** (*Musée du Cheval),* with its collection of international saddles, skeletons of famed thoroughbreds and hugely fascinating collection of stirrups, spurs and bits from all periods and all nations. Among the many unique exhibits look out for a foot-warmer stirrup, a pegleg stirrup, a lantern stirrup for doctors on night calls and a Japanese postman's bell-stirrup to warn of his approach.

Valençay

Set in its own romantic park close to the River Nahon, built on the remains of an 11th-century feudal fortress in the mid-16th century, this elegant château is essentially Renaissance, despite 17th- and 18th-century extensions and additions.

Valençay *is* Talleyrand. Born under a lucky star in

Outlined grimly against the sky, Saumur château inspires awe.

1754, this bishop, statesman, diplomat, socialite, wit, gastronome, man-of-letters and arch-opportunist successfully survived the French Revolution (as a refugee in America during its worst excesses), the *Directoire*, the First Empire, the Restoration and the 1830 revolution, serving as ambassador to London from 1830 to 1834; Talleyrand died in 1838 and is buried in the town where he is still affectionately remembered as its benefactor.

The château was bought by Talleyrand in 1803, on the orders of First Consul Bonaparte who wanted a showplace to impress friendly ambassadors and visiting heads of state. Talleyrand, his skilful, urbane foreign minister, was clearly the man to run it.

When Napoleon captured and deposed King Ferdinand VII of Spain and sparked off the Peninsular War, he chose Valençay as a gilded cage for the royal prisoner and packed him off there with his brother, uncle and suite. From 1808 to 1814 Talleyrand did all he could to make his "guests'" stay as painless as possible and succeeded admirably, for when the Spaniards finally returned home, they left Valençay tearfully.

The château **apartments,** furnished in Louis XVI and Empire styles, produce an atmosphere meaningful to modern visitors, reminding us vividly that Talleyrand himself limped through these very rooms less than a 150 years ago. On the first floor is the King's Room, occupied by Ferdinand VII, with its original furniture and some finely preserved wallpaper.

The **grounds** are full of surprises and worth exploring for their own sake. Near the entrance gates lies the 18th-century building converted by Talleyrand into an orangery and now a museum of Talleyrandiana. In it is a reconstruction of Talleyrand's bedroom in the château, a lifelike portrait of Ferdinand VII presented by him to Talleyrand and numerous mementoes of the great man, not forgetting a rather sad orthopaedic shoe for his club foot, the result of a childhood accident. Next to it stands the little theatre he had built for his Spanish guests' entertainment.

But, biggest surprise of all, there are animals—exotic

Villandry's gardens form a mosaic of geometric perfection.

birds, peacocks, flamingoes, zebras, deer and a camel—roaming free everywhere and even a row of colourful parrots.

Villandry

You'll see nothing like Villandry's French **Renaissance gardens** anywhere in the world. They're a unique,

historically and botanically accurate reconstruction of what the château's gardens could have looked like when it was built in 1532. Dating only from the early years of this century, it was all due to an enthusiastic and scholarly owner, Dr. Carvallo, whose family are still the proprietors.

Seen from the air, the geometric perfection and harmony of these gardens is breathtaking. You'll have an equally impressive view at ground-level, for the gardens are built on three separate levels, affording superb panoramic views.

You'll see perfect ranks of espalier-trained fruit trees; box- and yew-trees trimmed to perfection; evergreen hedges clipped and shaped into maddening mazes, complicated patterns or love-knots; cool, vine-covered arbours, fountains and canals in this stately but thrilling

complex. And it takes just five gardeners working year-round to keep it all going.

The kitchen garden, with its aesthetically planted vegetables is sheer delight. It will give you a new perspective on vegetables and perhaps even make your children think twice before leaving them on their plates! No tomatoes or potatoes here: they were unknown in Europe at the time.

The château itself, a pure Renaissance building in spite of the massive 14th-century keep curiously embedded in it (the remains of an earlier feudal fortress), is worth visiting for its fine collection of Spanish paintings and furniture.

And More Châteaux…

Beaugency

A fifteenth-century château built by Dunois, one of Joan of Arc's comrades-in-arms. Dwarfed by a towering 11th-century keep—reminder of the town's constant strategic importance. Captured four times by the English, retaken in 1429 by Joan of Arc. It houses an interesting museum of regional crafts.

Brissac

Despite a curious marriage of styles (15th–17th centuries), the general effect is outstanding. Owned by the Duc de Brissac, direct descendant of the 16th-century owner, it boasts an interesting collection of furniture, paintings, tapestries, one magnificently decorated ceiling and a resi-

Every curve in the road reveals another château (left, sumptuous Serrant); right: an amusing ceiling panel at Plessis-Bourré. **73**

dent ghost called "the Green Lady".

Gien
Overlooking the Loire, built in the 15th century by Anne de Beaujeu, daughter of Louis XI. Francis I, Louis XIV, Anne of Austria and Cardinal Mazarin briefly resided here. It now houses a unique International Museum of Hunting.

Le Lude
Once a medieval fortress guarding the River Loir. Fought over by English and French, rebuilt in the 15th and 16th centuries, it serves today as a dramatic setting for an historical waterside pageant (June–September) by over 300 costumed performers with a sound-and-light backing.

Le Plessis-Bourré
Impregnable but cosy island château in a huge moat. Built in the 15th century by royal minister Jean Bourré (who also built Langeais for Louis XI). Terraces below walls at moat level were for low-firing defensive artillery. Within, 30 remarkable, 15th-century humorously painted **ceiling panels.** Proverbs? Allegories? No one really knows.

Serrant
Mirrored in a romantic lake, apparently a Renaissance château but built later, between the 16th and 18th centuries. Its 18th-century owner bought Bonnie Prince Charlie two ships to help in his bid for the English throne. A painting in the richly stocked library commemorates the gift.

Sully-sur-Loire
A flock of ravenous ducks and swans in the moat add a light touch to this fortress-dwelling. Joan of Arc stayed here, an unwilling guest; Henry IV's minister Sully, its owner, retired to it in disgrace and died here. Remarkably preserved 14th-century chestnut-wood **timbers.** Superb views over the Loire from the battlements.

Ussé
All a fairy-tale castle should be, it's said to have inspired the author of *The Sleeping Beauty* and is a firm favourite with Japanese tourists. Built in the 15th, with 16th- and 17th-century additions, it possesses distinguished paintings and furniture. Beautiful gardens and a Renaissance chapel not to be missed.

What to Do

Off the Château Trail...

The Loire Valley is not all castles and churches. You could spend an entire holiday without touching a single one of them and still not see everything the region offers.

Those characteristic **"troglodyte" dwellings** are a case in point. Above or below ground, they're everywhere. You could never hope to cover them all. See them on the road from Tours to Langeais, at Vouvray and Rochecorbon, from Tours to Saumur; at Amboise between the château and manor-house of Clos-Lucé; at Montrichard; at Troo, where they're built into the rock one on top of the other—a maddeningly complicated ensemble; at Doué-la-Fontaine (Rue des Perrières); at Villaines-les-Rochers. And at Louresse-Rochemenier, near Doué,

One young couple sets off to a prehistoric start in married life.

visit an entire hamlet-in-the-rock and a peasant-crafts museum *(Musée troglodytique et paysan)*.

The **limestone caves** *(grottes pétrifiantes)* at Savonnières, near Tours, add an unusual note to a long list of caves and cellars. They communicate with Villandry's château through a one-mile-long natural passage, now partly blocked. The petrifying quality of dripping limestone particles is fully exploited here to produce extraordinary souvenirs in a matter of months. See also gigantic to tiny ammonite fossils found in the caves. Some are for sale. Around Saumur, miles of abandoned cave-quarries were taken over by mushroom-growers who created a thriving local industry. Many can be visited, but don't miss the one at Saint-Hilaire-Saint-Florent—just outside Saumur—the Mushroom Museum *(Musée du Champignon)*.

Saumur's surroundings are full of surprises: the massive dolmen at Bagneux is not the least of them. Over 65 feet long, 20 feet wide, standing over 6 feet high, it's one of France's major megalithic monuments. But its present-day setting is still more sur-prising, for it lies in the garden of a pleasant *bistrot*. Bring your own picnic, order a beer and eat at tables beside this prehistoric dolmen—a rare experience. Dolmen and menhir enthusiasts will find a lot more of them around Gennes, 15 kilometres west of Saumur.

Doué-la-Fontaine, also known as Doué-les-Roses, boasts a respectable **zoo.** Try its unique "snake safari", an expertly conducted tour with some impressive reptiles gliding freely around you. Strictly for snake-lovers. Don't miss Doué's unusual Arènes (arena) and the fine stone **windmill** as you drive into the town from Saumur. You'll see an even more typical Angevin windmill nearby on the road to Brissac, and you'll spot others on the skyline as you drive around Anjou.

Zoos make good breaks from châteaux for the children: besides Doué's, there is the Zoo de Montevran at Chaumont-sur-Tharonne (Sologne), and du Tertre Rouge at La Flèche (north of Angers).

A fascinating experience for young and old is the little vintage **steam railway** that runs in season from Chinon to Richelieu and back, with a stop half-way for local wine- and cheese-tasting. Visit amazing **Richelieu,** a "model" town built by the cardinal in 1631, described by La Fontaine as "the most beautiful village in the world".

Almost everywhere along the Loire's banks you'll be driving high on dyke-like roads, or **levées,** man-made ramparts, parts of them dating as far back as the 12th century, set up to contain the rising waters of a capricious Loire. Look out for numerous markers recording hair-raising former flood levels— some well above the road.

Even a delicate Anjou headdress can be too hot in summer.

Fairs, Festivals, Events

Loire Valley celebrations, often purely agricultural in origin, are now widely enjoyed by town- and country-dwellers alike—and by tourists.

May is the month for major national trade fairs (Tours, Saumur, Angers) and an excuse for side-amusements like mammoth fun-fairs (carnivals), open-air dances, food- and wine-tasting and so on. It's also a month when smaller, highly animated local fairs are held: asparagus fairs at Tigy and Vineuil, an *andouille* fair at Jargeau, a cheese fair at Valençay, all backed by sports events, 77 parades with floats and majorettes, dances and funfairs.

At Orléans, they celebrate Joan of Arc and National Liberation Day (May 7 and 8) in style with fireworks, folkloric and historic parades, illuminations.

In **June,** the Anjou Wines and Châteaux Air Rally and Saumur's flower parade draw enthusiastic crowds; Angers and Beaugency hold drama festivals; the exciting 24-hour Le Mans motor race takes place in mid-June. If you're there, don't miss Le Mans itself (Saint-Julien Cathedral, Gallo-Roman walls, Sainte-Jeanne-d'Arc Church, picturesque buildings in the old part of town). At the end of June, Touraine holds a music festival in an unusual setting—the Granges de Meslay—ancient farm buildings once owned by St. Martin's monastery of Marmoutier.

July is a peak month for tourist-orientated events: more concerts are held in Touraine and elsewhere; Doué-la-Fontaine's International Rose Show in its remarkable setting is a sight to be seen; the important Anjou Music, Dance and Operatic Festival attracts distinguished performers; comely wearers of Angevin headdresses parade at La Ménitré—a chance for some folkloric photography; Saumur's Cadre Noir performs at its *Carrousels;* Thésée-la-Romaine holds its wine fair and Amboise its annual town celebrations, enlivened by many period-costumed tradespeople.

August is Chinon's turn for its gargantuan celebrations: its streets and market "go medieval" with everything from troubadours and pedlars to tumblers and fire-eaters. Cheverny offers torchlit evocations of the hunt; Saint-Aignan holds regattas on the Cher.

Grape harvesting takes place in September and October but the vintage festivities run on well into the winter months; major wine fairs are held at Angers and at Azay-le-Rideau (January), at Selles-sur-Cher (April), Beaugency (October), Bourgueil (February, Easter Tuesday, second Tuesday in September).

A succession of agricultural fairs run from April to November, with everything from asparagus to geese, from chestnuts to goats, from garlic to cheese. Local fairs draw together friendly, often picturesque crowds.

Museums and Visits

There are more museums in and around the Loire Valley than you'll probably want to visit, but here's a list to help you choose. Museums are generally open from 10 a.m. to noon and from 2 to 4 p.m. and closed on Mondays or Tuesdays. Check with the local tourist office.

A moment in the river's history is immortalized in old faïence.

Archaeology. Blois, Châteaumeillant, Le Grand Pressigny, Orléans, Romorantin, Thésée-la-Romaine, Tours.

Fine arts. Angers, Blois, Orléans, Tours, Saumur (china).

Hunting and fishing. La Bussière (fishing), Cère-la-Ronde, Gien, Cheverny.

Illusionists. Exhibits at Blois devoted to Robert Houdin, the 19th-century scientist and illusionist, from whom the American magician Harry Houdini took his name.

Local history, folklore, crafts. Amboise, Châteauneuf-sur-Loire, Chinon, Beaugency, Les Ponts-de-Cé, Loches, Louresse-Rochemenier, Orléans, Plessis-lès-Tours, Romorantin, Saint-Laurent-de-la-Plaine, Tigy, Tours.

Military. Angers, La Flèche, Montsoreau, Saumur.

Natural history. Chaumont-sur-Tharonne, Doué-la-Fontaine, La Flèche (zoos), Angers, Ingrandes, Orléans.

Transport and cars. Amboise (postal), Briare, Le Mans, Montrichard, Villesavin.

Factory visits. Cointreau and slate-works at Angers, Poulain chocolates at Blois, Gien chinaworks, Combier at Saumur, innumerable wine cellars large and small (see p. 98).

Shopping

Shopping Hours

In general, shopping hours in France are from 8 or 9 a.m. to noon and from 2 to 7 p.m. Off-season and in winter, most shops tend to close earlier. Food-shops open on Sunday mornings. Department stores and most shops are closed on Monday mornings.

Where to Shop

Shops and department stores in the Loire Valley offer as wide a range of goods as you'll find anywhere in France or in Paris itself. Some of the shoes, umbrellas, linen articles and women's wear on display will quite probably be of local manufacture, though by no means cheap. Blois, Tours, Saumur and Angers all offer good facilities, as do small Loire towns like Amboise or Loches. But for really sophisticated shopping, Orléans takes a lot of beating.

If you're returning home to a non-Common Market country, ask about the possibility of a refund of the value-added tax (*TVA*, see p. 119) in stores.

Riding Gear and Hunting Gifts

Naturally in Orléans, capital of the Sologne, hunting, fishing and riding take pride of place. Riding kits for young and old are undoubtedly among the best buys. Boots, jackets, breeches, hats and saddles priced to suit every pocket are among the cheapest you're likely to find in France. For riders and non-riders alike, there's a lavish choice of unusual equestrian gifts, modest or extravagant, from keyrings and ashtrays to horse-bit bracelets and belt buckles, *couturier* headscarves and ivory tiepins.

Between Orléans and Tours you'll find an especially large concentration of gunsmiths and dealers in hunting and fishing gear. Shotguns come in a wide international range, and leather accessories (cartridge belts, game-bags) are also worth looking at. Fishing tackle tends to be of the elaborate, expensive kind, not worth investing in unless you're out to do some serious fishing.

In the hunting-gift category, you'll be offered deer feet turned into such mundane objects as coat- or gunracks, salad servers, bottle openers and nutcrackers. And if you can't bag a wild boar, you can always take home a furry toy one complete with felt tusks or, better still, a genuine stuffed one. In this part of the world, there are almost as many taxidermists as there are châteaux.

In the dressing booth at a local fair, demoiselles *compare notes.*

Chinaware

Authentic local crafts are tending to die out everywhere, but the Loire Valley still comes up with some exciting surprises. For a start, there's a highly flourishing china and pottery industry. The famous Gien *faïence* (china) has its own distinctive

and highly attractive motifs, many of them still hand-painted today. It's now found all over France, but is much cheaper bought locally. In former days, this china was laboriously transported down the Loire on barges travelling in single-file convoys to avoid treacherous sandbanks.

The Gien factory at Place de la Victoire (founded in 1821 by an Englishman) sells almost perfect "seconds" very cheaply, while a collection of tempting china shops around the Avenue du Général Leclerc offers a vast choice of reasonably priced original gifts and souvenirs.

You can buy colourful plates bearing those familiar royal arms—salamanders, porcupines and other motifs to hang on the wall, as well as eight- or twelve-person dinner services.

Among the china you'll notice a totally different, more robust glazed pottery—the *grès de Touraine,* no less famous and very popular with lovers of country-style designs. Produced mainly on a smaller scale, often

Take home a quaint souvenir of the 'good old days'—or a mask.

by individual artisans, it offers unlimited varieties of attractive jars, punchbowl sets, dishes, cups and jugs, not to mention special plates for serving snails and little pots for the renowned local *rillettes* (see p. 91).

Medallions

Sober Saumur has been manufacturing religious medallions and rosaries since the 17th century. The output of souvenir metal keyrings now far exceeds that of devotional objects, though Saumur designers and manufacturers are still proud purveyors of gold and other medals to the Vatican. The most popular local keyring motif shows a horse and rider from Saumur's famous riding school. Major châteaux are also represented in this form, and you'll find them in souvenir shops throughout the Loire.

Masks

In total contrast, Saumur boasts Europe's largest carnival-mask factory. On sale everywhere during carnival time (they export all over the world, including to the big Mardi Gras capitals like New Orleans, Munich and Basle,

Switzerland), their masks are available year-round in Saumur. Irresistible to children of all ages, they make amusing and original presents.

Wines and Delicacies

Local wines (see p. 95), renowned but nevertheless not so commonly found as Burgundies or Bordeaux wines, make most appreciated gifts—if you can part with them. Spirits and liqueurs are naturally **83** also worth buying to take home (see p. 97). So are such delicacies as stuffed prunes from Tours, Sologne honey, Orléans' *cotignac*—an attractively presented quince jelly—and hosts of unnamed individual chocolate and sweetmeat specialities you'll want to try for yourself.

Woodwork
In the pure artisan class, look out for objects made with vine branches—side-tables, lamps and chandeliers, coat-racks or corkscrews made largely in the Saumur-Angers region, but available everywhere. With barrels all too often replaced by glass vats, coopers *(tonneliers)* are a dying race, but some manage to survive. You can buy a barrel old or new, large or small for use as a table base, a bar, a seat or whatever you fancy. They're not exactly cheap, though supermarkets sometimes sell advantageous 10-litre (about 2½ gallons) wine-filled barrels complete with tap.

Wrought Ironwork
Blacksmiths, once found in every village, are now rare. There's still some shoeing work, especially around the Sologne, but the survivors have gradually converted to making decorative and expensive fire-irons or film-epic-style chandeliers. Keep an eye open for such signs as *ferronnerie d'art* (wrought ironwork). It costs nothing to have a look at what's offered, and you just might pick up a bargain.

Wickerwork
Wickerwork of local manufacture using local raw materials (mainly from the town of Thouarce near Angers) is something else you will come across. The village of Villaines-les-Rochers, near Chinon, is peopled by basket-makers and also worth a visit for its "troglodyte" dwellings.

Antiques
You'll discover plenty of antique shops in most town centres as you explore them. In smaller places such as Amboise, Langeais, Azay-le-Rideau and Loches, they're conveniently close to the châteaux. Though most of them do sell some local objects and furniture, a lot of their stock is necessarily "imported". Prices are not especially higher than elsewhere, except for reproduction copperware, that tends to be exorbitant. Best buys here are old china

plates, often refreshingly cheap. Dealers are always open to bargaining. And if you enjoy a good haggle, don't miss the weekly Saturday flea market at Angers (Place Louis Imbach).

Shopping Tips

Prices vary according to the class of shop. Boutiques will clearly charge more than a chain store. But whatever you're buying, whether it's a dress or a shotgun, a riding outfit or a piece of china, it's always worth looking at one or two shops stocking similar articles to establish a basic price comparison. Sales (soldes) are held in January and July, and French shops usually stick to those periods.

When making substantial purchases in a non-department store, you can suggest a small discount (un rabais). China shops often give you the choice between a free gift and a cash reduction, but there's no hard-and-fast rule about discounts in France.

And don't forget that certain items, like Angers' world-famous Cointreau liqueur and those tempting French perfumes can be bought more cheaply at airport duty-free shops or cross-Channel ferries.

Sports and Leisure Activities

In the Loire Valley you'll find yourself indulging in a good deal of mental gymnastics trying to remember dates, names, styles and which king built what or lived where. But if you're making a real holiday of it, take a break now and then from sheer history to enjoy some of the tempting outdoor activities the region has to offer.

Walking

This is a perfect year-round activity and a pleasant way to get to know the Loire Valley. Whether you choose to hike through the forests of the Sologne, stroll all over Orléans' huge floral park or wander at leisure along river banks and country lanes in Touraine and Anjou, you'll find the going ideal for all the family, young and not-so-young. Sensible walking shoes and a detailed local road map are all you'll need.

Forests around Orléans, Blois, Amboise and Chinon are excellent for walking or picnicking.

Cycling

This is a relaxed way to do some leisurely sightseeing. **85**

Whether you're staying in town or country the open road is always easily accessible. You can cover a lot of ground in one day or in a week with a hired bicycle (see p. 107).

Horseriding

Riding is probably the most popular year-round outdoor activity in the Loire Valley.

Centres équestres or *clubs hippiques* (riding centres or clubs) are to be found absolutely everywhere.

Riding is a fairly expensive sport the world over, and the Loire Valley is no exception. But a reduction is often available for children, and an hour's pleasurable horse-back ride should not leave you penniless. Try and fix in advance as demand is heavy. Private instruction is usually available. Local tourist offices will supply information on the riding facilities in their own area.

Hunting and Shooting

In the autumn and winter months, hunting takes pride of place. Roads, fields and forests swarm with hopeful nimrods and their dogs. But unless you're lucky enough to be a VIP guest of the President of France or know somebody with a private shoot, you won't find it too easy to get a shot at some French game.

If you enjoy the spectacle of a traditional hunt and happen to be in the Forêt de Boulogne on a Tuesday or a Saturday between mid-October and mid-April, you might catch a glimpse of the Cheverny hunt in full cry, horns blowing and hounds baying (see p. 59).

It's possible for a visitor or group to ride with a local hunt. Prior arrangements can be made through the French State Tourist Office in your country or by direct application to the hunt concerned.

For marksmen there are skeet and trapshooting clubs throughout the Loire Valley, with guns usually available for hire.

Fishing

Fishing is altogether an easier and cheaper proposition than hunting. You can obtain a licence on the spot through the local fishing association *(Société de Pêche)* or you can first enquire at any local tourist office. The local association will also let you know where you can fish and generally advise you on baits and

86

other details. Cast- and fly-fishing licences are obviously more expensive than straightforward rod-and-line ones. In some cases it's possible to obtain a one-day licence. Do not fish wherever you see the notice *pêche interdite* (no fishing).

There's an excellent fishing reserve at Luzillé, near Chenonceaux: you can fish carp and tench there between May and October.

Salmon is now comparatively rare in the Loire and reserved for full-time fishermen who stretch nets almost from bank to bank to ensure a reasonable if less sporting annual catch. But there are still plenty of pike and pike-perch to be caught.

The pools of the Sologne and the Loire Valley rivers offer a respectable variety of

At Saumur's annual Carrousel, a historical pageant comes to life.

The Loire can be treacherous, but not for shore fishermen.

fish ranging from carp, chub, roach, eel, gudgeon, bleak, trout and bream to perch, black bass, mullet and shad.

Swimming

There are good, up-to-date open-air and indoor swimming pools throughout the Loire Valley. Some of the larger campsites have pools, and many spots along the Loire and other local rivers offer well-equipped sand beaches with swimming and boating facilities *(plans d'eau aménagés)*. Entrance fees are usually charged both to swimming pools and river beaches (for rates, see p. 104). For swimming, stick to officially marked bathing areas, especially in the River Loire. Despite its placid appearance it's full of treacherous undercurrents which could prove fatal to anyone rash enough to ignore them.

Boating and Sailing

You'll find a diversity of craft available, from motorboats and simple sailing-boats to canoes, *pédalos* and rowing-boats. The Base du Lac de

Loire at Vineuil near Blois— a vast modern recreational and camping complex—offers all of these at the same time, but elsewhere you'll find at least one or more of these facilities along the Loire, the Cher, the Indre, the Vienne or the Maine.

In boating as in swimming, stick to officially marked areas *(plans d'eau)*, for in addition to currents there are sandbanks.

Tennis

There's no lack of tennis facilities. The French have taken to this sport in a big way in recent years. Even small villages often boast a court. There are hourly court-charge and season-ticket possibilities, and tennis lessons are available on major camp-sites and at most organized clubs. Generally speaking, you'll find hard rather than grass courts.

Golf

There are golf courses at Vi-glain near Orléans, at Ballan-Miré near Tours (18 holes) and at Saint-Jean-des-Mau-vrets near Angers. Some château-hotels have their own private courses. You'll find no lack of mini-golf facilities.

Wining and Dining

If the sights of the Loire Valley are a feast for your eyes, its gastronomy will be no less of a feast for the palate. This, after all, is the land of François Rabelais, the 16th-century Benedictine monk, satirist, humourist and epicure, whose immortal literary characters, Gargantua, the giant king, and his son Pantagruel, both enjoyed a lusty capacity for food and drink. Their legendary banquets have given way to a gastronomy at once robust and refined, using the best of everything the region has to offer: A wide range of cooked-meat products from Touraine and Anjou, game from Sologne, fish from the Loire, fruit and vegetables from Touraine, along with asparagus, strawberries, mushrooms—wild or cultivated—liqueurs from Anjou and a selection of magnificent cheeses—all go to make some of the tastiest yet most unpretentious dishes to be found in France.*

---

* For a comprehensive glossary of French culinary terms and how to order wine, ask your bookshop for the Berlitz EUROPEAN MENU READER.

Touraine, the Garden of France, is noted for fine food and wine.

A *charcuterie* (derived from *chair cuite*—"cooked meat") is a shop that primarily boasts a vast variety of pork products—also called *charcuterie*—usually made on the premises and ranging from succulent sausages to savoury cured hams and pâtés. Found throughout the Loire Valley, these French-style delicatessens offer an unbelievable selection of delicacies, varying according to season. They may also offer salads, seafood dishes, roasts and relishes.

Charcuterie

Here are just a few of the items you'll see on menus or in *charcuterie* windows:

Andouillette: seasoned, aromatic sausage made from tripe, served grilled or fried.

Galantine, ballotine: made with a variety of pressed meats, mainly fowl and game.

Rillettes: minced duck, goose or pork cooked for hours to a creamy consistency in its own fat and served chilled in earthenware pots; an appetizing starter or sandwich filler.

Rillons: small-to-medium chunks of pork breast, eaten hot or cold, usually as a starter.

Pâté, terrine: often an exquisite preparation of ground goose or duck liver (like the renowned *pâté de foie gras*), they may also be similar to a meat loaf made of one or several kinds of meat.

Some Regional Specialities

Try the famous *andouillettes* from Tours. Finely pricked all round and grilled over a charcoal or vine-branch fire, these tripe sausages are delicious. Angers jealously boasts the same speciality.

From Tours again come the tasty *rillettes*. In restaurants, they're served as starters in attractive, little glazed earthenware pots. In *charcuteries,* you buy *rillettes* by weight. (For a picnic, 50 grams [1³/₄ oz.] per person is ample.) It's delicious spread on crisp, French bread. You'll find *rillettes* everywhere, as well as those chunky pork morsels known as *rillons*.

Fish Delights

Fish dishes are part of the local culinary tradition: salmon and pike being featured, though shad, grey mullet, carp, trout, pike-perch, bream and eel are no less appreciated.

All of these fish are caught in the Loire and its affluents, in the River Maine or in the ponds of Sologne. Most of them are prepared very simply—either sautéed or poached—often served with *beurre blanc* (white butter sauce). A remarkable blend of simple ingredients (butter, **91** shallots, vinegar and white wine), the sauce was invented by a certain Mother Clémence, from Anjou, one of those many local cooks who helped make Angevin cuisine justly famous.

Pike-perch (or walleyed pike) is especially common in the Loire and often replaces salmon and pike on the menu. Less sought after, in experienced hands it still makes a highly memorable dish with its *beurre blanc* accompaniment. Also try a *matelote d'anguille*, a speciality (in Touraine and Anjou) of eel stewed in red wine, the latter being preferably a vintage Chinon or Bourgueil.* *Bouilleture d'anguilles*, eel cooked in cream, is more exclusively Angevin. Trout, carp or pike *à la Chambord* are frequently seen on menus. The fish, stuffed with fish purée and truffles, is elaborately garnished with a variety of vegetables. *Quenelles* are exquisite dumplings, generally of pike, often presented on their own with an aromatic crayfish sauce—all the flavour but nary a

bone. There's also shad, served with *beurre blanc* on a bed of sorrel cooked in cream. These are just a few of the greatest local dishes.

But don't turn your nose up at a *petite friture de la Loire*. Eaten in a modest *bistrot* by the water's edge, washed down with a glass or two of chilled Saumur wine, even this plateful of small, deep-fried fish will be something you'll long remember.

Meat

Meat, as everywhere in France, is often of excellent quality. *Entrecôte* (rib-eye steak), *filet de bœuf* (strip steak) or *escalope de veau* (veal scallop) appear regularly on menus.

Try local specialities like *cul de veau à l'angevine* (veal rump in a rich sauce with vegetables) and *noisette de porc aux pruneaux* (pork tenderloin with prunes).

Local poultry is always outstanding and never seems to have that "mass production" taste. Sample some of these chicken dishes: *fricassée de volaille* (chicken fricassee), *coq au Bourgueil, Vouvray* or *Chinon* (chicken stewed in wine of one of these localities) or *coquelet à la moutarde* or *à l'estragon* (spring

* A gourmet hint: when ordering any dish prepared with wine, you'll be enhancing its quality if you drink the same wine that went into its preparation.

chicken with mustard or tarragon sauce). Duck abounds in the Loire Valley. Almost every farm has a pond, and you'll see hordes of ducks roaming free around farmyards. Local restaurateurs need look no further for their raw materials.

Cheeses
In this supermarket age, farm-produced cheeses are gradually disappearing in the face of competition from large-scale producers. But you can still find them sometimes in village grocers' or if you ask at a farm where they keep goats. Goat's-milk cheese is very much a Loire Valley speciality, as a visit to any supermarket will convince you. Among the best-known goats' cheeses you're likely to find and taste on restaurant cheeseboards, are the Sainte-Maure, Saint-Loup, Valençay and Selles-sur-Cher (matured in a coating of salt and charcoal ash). Olivet, a small, round cheese matured in vinebranch ashes, is sold or served wrapped in walnut leaves. You'll find these and others, such as the *chèvre de Loches* and the blue-veined Vendôme, almost everywhere. As for the *crémet d'Angers,* a fresh,

white creamy cheese, try it as a dessert, sprinkled with sugar.

Desserts

Desserts on the whole are unexceptional: restaurateurs nowadays have too little time to do more than "buy in" fruit and ice-cream. Pastries make some of the best desserts. One you're almost sure to try is *tarte Tatin*—a tart baked crust-side up (like apple cobbler)—named after two sisters from Sologne who first made it famous. A *soufflé au Cointreau,* flavoured with orange liqueur, is another restaurant standby from Angers to Orléans. Icecreams and *sorbets* (sherbets) can range from mediocre to good.

Don't limit pastry-sampling to restaurants. Loire Valley people have a sweet tooth, and you'll find an ample choice of meringues, *mille-feuilles* (napoleons) and cream cakes in every town or country *pâtisserie* (cake and pastry shop). Fruit tarts are usually the best value for your money. Incidentally, *pâtisseries* are often tea-shops (*salons de thé*) as well, and good places to enjoy a quiet cup of tea in dainty surroundings.

Restaurants

Most restaurants offer one or two set menus *(menu à prix fixe),* in addition to an à la carte menu. Some smaller places offer just a take-it-or-leave-it fixed-price meal.

Cheaper meals often run to three courses, with or without wine, but with service always included.

More expensive menus stretch to four or even five courses, but hardly ever include wine.

Restaurants are legion in the Valley of the Loire but, as everywhere in France, have no "official" grading. Unless they already boast a star awarded by a gastronomic guide or enjoy some other, similar rating, it's not always easy to tell whether they're good, bad or indifferent. One way is to note what vegetables are offered on the set-price menus. A conscientious restaurateur who takes the trouble to prepare local fresh vegetables or products like runner beans, fresh asparagus, salsify, artichoke, mushrooms, chestnuts etc. deserves your confidence. A fair crowd of French or local-looking customers is also a promising sign.

Unless you're after a quick, unimaginative meal, beware

of those establishments offering *steack-frites* (steak-and-chips) menus 365 days of the year.

Wines

The Loire Valley was naturally predestined to become a great wine-producing region. The mildness of its climate, its gentle and well-exposed slopes, the nature of its soil, chalky or alluvial, the handy proximity of rivers for easy transport—all these factors have contributed to make it one of the top wine districts of France.

Rosé and Red Wines

Of all the Loire wines, the rosés d'Anjou are perhaps the most commonly seen and the most popular outside France. Refreshing, light and fruity, served slightly chilled, they're at their best with starters or with a tasty local goat's cheese. While usually accompanying fowl and veal dishes, you could drink *vin rosé* right through a meal.

You'll find, in addition, a variety of equally well-known and delectables rosés, worth sampling on the spot or taking home with you: cabernet d'Anjou and cabernet de Saumur; slightly sparkling (*pétillant*) or even bubbly

(*mousseux*) rosé d'Anjou for those who like their wine fizzy; the excellent dry rosés de Touraine, which comprise Azay-le-Rideau, Mesland,

Pop! Sparkling wine adds zest to any event—grand or modest.

Amboise and Touraine (*pétillant);* and finally the coteau-du-Loir and rosé de Loire.

Supreme among the red wines are Bourgueil, Saint-Nicolas-de-Bourgueil and Chinon. The first two have a fruity, raspberry taste, while Chinon will remind you of violets. Deep, rich red in colour, delicate and mellow, they're best drunk with game, grilled meats or meat dishes in sauce, but are just as good with pork and fowl, and with cheeses. They are always served at cellar temperature.

Fruity or smooth, other distinguished reds like Anjou rouge, gamay d'Anjou, Saumur rouge and Saumur-Champigny are less massively produced. Try them locally.

White Wines
For their variety and remarkable quality, white wines are the acknowledged stars of the Loire's vineyards. Dry, semi-dry, mellow or even sweet according to vintage, the wines of Vouvray (exported as early as the 12th century), Montlouis and Saumur, are outstanding. Whether still and dry, slightly sparkling or champagne-style, they are always deliciously light, fruity and refreshing. Try them with starters, *rillettes* and *rillons, foie gras* or oysters and with all fish dishes and desserts.

The white wines of Anjou, at once mellow and lusty, are in a class of their own. Delicately straw-coloured, with a tinge of green, they're really tempting just to look at. Try wines from the coteaux du Layon (especially the outstanding Bonnezeaux and Quarts de Chaume), the coteaux de l'Aubance, coteaux de Saumur and coteaux de la Loire (in particular Savennières, Coulée de Serrant and Roche aux Moines). Drink these wines as an aperitif or enjoy them with starters, hot or cold, with fish or anything in a *beurre blanc* sauce and with blue cheese. These Loire Valley whites have the added quality of aging well.

Though not, strictly speaking, produced within the Loire Valley itself, two white wines you're very likely to come across are muscadet (coteau de Loire and Sèvres-et-Maine) and Sancerrois (Pouilly-sur-Loire, Pouilly fumé, Menetou-Salon, Quincy, Reuilly and Sancerre, the last five developed from Sauvignon stock and of exceptional quality).

Wine-Hunting

If you enjoy wine-hunting, keep your eyes open around Orléans for Meung-sur-Loire's red Gris Meunier, which was Louis XI's favourite, or the equally red Saint-Ay, whose vineyards once belonged to Henri IV. You'll also find wines from Valençay, Cheverny, côtes de Gien, coteaux de Châteaumeillant and coteaux de Vendômois, all produced in lesser quantities, but locally available.

When eating out, don't feel compelled to order bottled wine every time. The quality of open wine in the Loire Valley is generally high, and a simple *carafe* or *pichet* of

Wine-guild official, right, pays enthusiastic homage to Bacchus; roadside stand to quench thirsts.

local *rosé*, red or white can be as satisfying to drink—and cheaper.

Liqueurs and Brandies

Locally produced liqueurs and brandies *(eau-de-vie)* won't disappoint you either: there's hazelnut *(noisette)* liqueur from Orléans; orange liqueur, the world-famous *Cointreau*, made in Angers; Saumur's own orange cordial, *Combier; Guignolet*, Anjou's very own aperitif or afternoon drink, made from soft, plump cherries. Try it the way the local people drink it—with a dash of *kirsch* (cherry brandy).

Wine Cellars

Unless you're very careful, touring in the Loire Valley could become one long series of wine-tasting. Temptation lurks everywhere; you'll see cave after cave in those roadside hillocks of *tuffeau* stone, hundreds of them, some several miles deep, many of them ancient quarries with huge, excavated halls, all burrowing their way into the tufa.

Some cellars have set up museums where you'll see huge, centuries-old wooden presses and old vineyard implements. Don't miss the one at Bourgueil (Cave Touristique de la Dive Bouteille). There's wine-tasting there, too, as everywhere else. The fascinating Musée des Vins de Touraine (Wine Museum of Touraine), right in the middle of Tours (Celliers Saint-Julien, 16, rue Nationale), is worth seeing for its setting alone. It's housed in

Cellarman inspects his treasured stocks in a cool, converted cave.

the original 13th-century wine cellars of an ancient abbey, Saint-Julien, but surprisingly, for once, no wine-tasting here.

These museums and certain privately owned *caves* charge modest entrance fees, but in most cases entry and wine-tasting are absolutely free, even if a tip is sometimes expected. There's no obligation to buy anything, though you're welcome to do so. You'll find on-the-spot prices extremely reasonable.

Other Beverages

The French are keen on mineral water. Some, like Vichy, are touted for their curative powers and have a distinctly medicinal taste, while others, like Perrier, are fizzy and refreshing.

Those who wish to forego wine and liquor for a beer between meals will find good French *bière*. Tea and coffee are of passable quality, the latter rather strong, often somewhat bitter and never served with cream.

Breakfast

With all the fuss the French make over noon and evening meals, breakfast is rather unimportant, just a little something to tide one over until the time has come for a multicourse *déjeuner*. The *petit déjeuner* usually consists of only *café au lait* (white coffee) served with bread, crescent rolls, jam and butter.

To Help You Order...

Could we have a table?
Do you have a set-price menu?
I'd like a/an/some...

	Avez-vous une table?
	Avez-vous un menu à prix fixe?
	J'aimerais...

beer	**une bière**	mineral water	**de l'eau minérale**
butter	**du beurre**		
bread	**du pain**	potatoes	**des pommes de terre**
coffee	**un café**		
dessert	**un dessert**	salad	**une salade**
fish	**du poisson**	sandwich	**un sandwich**
fruit	**un fruit**	soup	**de la soupe**
glass	**un verre**	sugar	**du sucre**
ice-cream	**une glace**	tea	**du thé**
meat	**de la viande**	(iced) water	**de l'eau (glacée)**
menu	**la carte**		
milk	**du lait**	wine	**du vin**

...and Read the Menu

agneau	lamb	jambon	ham
ail	garlic	langue	tongue
alose	shad	lapin	rabbit
artichauts	artichoke	lièvre	hare
asperges	asparagus	macédoine	fruit salad
aubergines	eggplant	de fruits	
betterave	beet	marcassin	young boar
bifteck	steak	médaillon	tenderloin steak
bœuf	beef	melon	melon
brème	bream		(cantaloupe)
brochet	pike	mulet	grey mullet
caille	quail	moutarde	mustard
canard	duck	navets	turnips
caneton	duckling	nouilles	noodles
carottes	carrots	oie	goose
carpe	carp	oignons	onions
cervelle	brains	perdreau	young partridge
chèvre	goat	perdrix	partridge
chou	cabbage	petits pois	peas
chou-fleur	cauliflower	pigeonneau	young squab
choux de	brussels	pintade	guinea fowl
Bruxelles	sprouts	pommes	apples
coq	chicken	porc	pork
concombre	cucumber	poule	stewing fowl
côtelettes	chops, cutlet	poulet	chicken
courgettes	baby marrow	pruneaux	prunes
	(zucchini)	prunes	plums
dinde,	turkey	radis	radishes
dindonneau		raisins	grapes
endive	chicory	ris de veau	sweetbreads
	(endive)	rognons	kidneys
épaule	shoulder	sandre	pike-perch
épinards	spinach	sanglier	boar
escalope	scallop	saucisse/	sausage
faisan	pheasant	saucisson	
flageolets	beans	saumon	salmon
foie	liver	sorbet	water-ice
fraises	strawberries		(sherbet)
framboises	raspberries	truffes	truffles
gigot	leg	truite	trout
100 haricots verts	string beans	veau	veal

How to Get There

If the choice of ways to go is bewildering, the complexity of fares and regulations can be downright stupefying. A reliable travel agent, up to date on the latest zigs and zags, can suggest which plan is best for your timetable and budget.

From Great Britain

BY AIR. The main international airport serving the Loire Valley, at Tours, is linked by regular flights from London (Gatwick). There are also some flights from Gatwick to Poitiers and from London (Heathrow) to Nantes. A much greater choice of flights is available from London, provincial and Irish points to Paris. Air connections from Paris to Tours and the Loire towns are virtually non-existent, but it is worth looking into the fly-drive packages offered by various airlines operating out of Paris, with the use of a car included in the price of the air fare.

Scheduled airlines offer reduced excursion fares if you:
- fly at night in summer
- stay a certain number of days at your destination
- are under 22 years of age
- are a full-time student under 26

Freedom Fares offer savings to those who stay six days to one month, and are suitable if you want to visit several destinations during your visit to France. Also worth considering is the **Euro-Budget Excursion,** offering around 50% reduction. For Paris, the minimum stay is two days, for the rest of France, ten days; maximum stay is three months (no stopovers).

Charter Flights and Package Tours (including flight, hotel and board): A large number of tour operators offer holidays in the Loire Valley in summer and, to a much lesser extent, in winter. Prices vary enormously, depending largely on type of transport and standard of hotel accommodation. On the whole, these arrangements offer extremely good value.

BY ROAD. During the summer, when ferry space is at a premium, be sure you have a firm reservation. Here's how you can go:

By car ferry: the principal routes link Dover and Folkestone with Calais, Boulogne and Dunkirk; also Newhaven–Dieppe, Weymouth–Cherbourg, Southampton–Le Havre, Southampton–Cherbourg; Plymouth–Roscoff; and Rosslare, Ireland, with Le Havre and Cherbourg.

The **hovercraft** from Ramsgate or Dover to Calais takes about 35 minutes and costs around the same price as the ferry.

Once in France, British motorists usually need some time to become accustomed to driving on the right. There are good road connections to the principal resort areas of the Loire Valley.

BY BUS. Regular services go from London to Paris (via Calais) and from Manchester, Oldham and Rochdale (via Boulogne). The buses leave Victoria Station in London four times a week using the night crossing from Dover.

Europabus offers direct seasonal services from London to Paris, from where you can continue your journey to the Loire Valley.

BY RAIL. British and French Railways offer London-to-Paris service via Gatwick and Le Touquet or via Southend and Le Touquet with a possibility of overnight carriages from London. Ask for expert advice about the most economical rail tickets available.

Inter-Rail Card is a fixed-rate ticket for one month's unlimited second-class rail travel throughout most of Europe, including France, available to anyone under 26 and senior citizens over 65 (Inter-Rail-S), regardless of nationality.

From North America

Daily non-stop flights go to Paris from more than a dozen major U.S. and Canadian cities. Many smaller cities have daily connecting flights to either of Paris' airports.

Although you can get to Paris in four hours from New York or Washington, DC, on the Concorde, normal jet planes take about seven hours but cost a lot less. You can save by booking one of the following special fares:

- The 14- to 45-day **Excursion Fare** may be booked and ticketed at any time. This fare is not subject to any cancellation fees, but does change in price according to season of travel.

- The **APEX** fare must be booked and paid for 21 days prior to departure and is subject to a cancellation penalty unless you have a medical certificate. The ticket is good from 7 to 120 days and no stop-overs are permitted.

- **Executive Fares** offer extra service and attention during flights for the price of a one-way ticket plus a small extra charge. Stop-overs are permitted.

Charter Flights and Package Tours are available through airlines and travel agents. You'll also find charter flights organized by private organizations, companies or church groups.

The ITX (Inclusive Tour Excursion) lets you book only 7 days ahead for your 7- to 45-day stay. You can prolong your stay by up to 45 days for a reasonable fee. There's also an added fee if you plan additional stops.

Visitors from outside Europe may travel on the **Eurailpass,** a flat-rate unlimited mileage ticket, valid for first-class rail travel anywhere in Western Europe outside Great Britain. **Eurail Youthpass** is similar to the Eurailpass, but offers second-class travel at a cheaper rate to anyone under 26.

When to Go

If you're counting on plenty of sunshine and warm, balmy evenings, you'd be advised to go in the summer period, for the Loire Valley doesn't enjoy particularly good weather in the winter as a rule. Late spring and early autumn are considered the best times of all: it's then that the countryside is at its most beautiful.

Following are some average monthly temperatures:

	J	F	M	A	M	J	J	A	S	O	N	D
°F	44	45	57	59	71	73	76	78	68	66	50	47
°C	7	7	14	15	22	23	24	26	20	19	10	8

Planning Your Budget

To give you an idea of what to expect, here's a list of average prices in French francs (F). They can only be approximate, however, as inflation in France, as elsewhere, creeps relentlessly up.

Airport transfer. Taxi from Saint-Symphorien airport to Tours 25 F.

Baby-sitters. 20–25 F per hour.

Bicycle hire. 25–30 F per day, plus deposit.

Bus services. Orléans–Blois 20 F, Tours–Angers 25 F.

Camping. *Two-star site:* 5 F per person (half-price for children under 7), 4 F for tent space. *Four-star site:* 12 F per person, 6 F for tent space.

Car hire. *Renault 14 GTL* 110 F per day, 1.30 F per km., 1,350 F per week with unlimited mileage. *Renault 5 4dr* 135 F per day, 1.35 F per km., 1,800 F per week with unlimited mileage. *Peugeot 505 SR* 170 F per day, 2.00 F per km., 2,420 F per week with unlimited mileage. Add 17.6% tax.

Château visits. 4–12 F.

Cigarettes (packet of 20). French 4.50 F, foreign 7 F.

Entertainment. Cinema 10–25 F, discotheque (admission and first drink) 20–50 F, nightclub (admission and first drink) 30–50 F.

Guides. 350 F for an eight-hour day (plus lunch), 250 F for half a day, 250–300 F for an evening.

Hairdressers. *Man's* haircut 25–40 F. *Woman's* haircut about 50 F, shampoo and set or blow-dry 40–80 F, permanent wave about 120 F.

Hotels (double room with bath, summer season—not including breakfast). ****L from 300 F, **** 100–300 F, *** 120–200 F, ** 50–150 F, *40–75 F.

Meals and drinks. Continental breakfast 10–25 F, lunch (in fairly good establishment) 30–80 F, dinner 40–100 F, bottle of wine 20–50 F, carafe 10–20 F, beer 3–6 F, soft drink 2.50–6 F, coffee 1.50–4 F, cognac 5–10 F.

Sports. Entrance fee to swimming pools/river beaches 6–10 F (reductions for children). One-day fishing licence 15 F. Tennis 20–40 F per hour. Golf, green fee about 100 F, caddies 65 F, equipment 45 F.

Youth hostels. 10–25 F per day.

BLUEPRINT for a Perfect Trip

An A-Z Summary of Practical Information and Facts

Contents

A star (*) following an entry indicates that relevant prices are to be found on p. 104.

Listed after some basic entries is the appropriate French translation, usually in the singular, plus a number of phrases that should help you when seeking assistance.

Although every effort has been made to ensure the accuracy of the information contained in this book, changes will inevitably occur, and we would be pleased to hear of any new developments.

ACCOMMODATION★. See also CAMPING. France offers an immense variety of hotel accommodation to suit every taste and pocket. The Loire Valley is particularly well endowed with modest but comfortable establishments, many with first-rate restaurants.

Hotels. These are officially classified into five categories by the Commissariat Central du Tourisme. Room prices, fixed according to amenities, size and to the hotel's star rating, must be posted visibly at reception desks and behind each room door. Hotels marked *NN (Nouvelles Normes)* have been reclassified and correspond to current standards of comfort.

Note: Hôtel de Ville is not a hotel, but the town hall.

Châteaux-Hôtels de France. A chain covering the whole of France, and offering several tempting possibilities in the Loire Valley, notably in Touraine. All are four-star establishments.

Relais de campagne. A similar chain offering a wider variety of hotels in country settings, from two- to four-star establishments. Some are genuine, old-time stagecoach inns. Both *châteaux-hôtels* and *relais* are listed jointly in a free booklet published annually.

Logis de France; Auberges rurales. Government-sponsored hotels, often on the outskirts or outside of towns. *Logis de France* are in the one- and two-star bracket; *auberges rurales* are three- or four-star establishments. A *Guide des Logis de France* is produced annually.

Gîtes de France; Gîtes ruraux. Officially sponsored, furnished holiday accommodation houses, apartments or rooms, with standards and prices officially controlled. Especially developed in Anjou. Rental costs are inclusive of all charges.

Auberges de jeunesse (youth hostels). There are about ten in the Loire Valley. Your national youth hostel association can give you all the details, or contact the Fédération Unie des Auberges de Jeunesse:

6, rue de Mesnil, 75116 Paris; tel. 261.84.03

Syndicats d'initiative (see TOURIST INFORMATION OFFICES) throughout the Loire Valley have their own additional lists of unofficial local accommodation.

a double/single room with/without bath	**une chambre à deux lits/à un lit avec/sans bains**
What's the rate per night?	**Quel est le prix pour une nuit?**

AIRPORT★ *(aéroport)*. See also p. 101. The airport at Saint-Symphorien, near Tours, is linked with London (Gatwick). (If you arrive at one of the Paris airports, you'll have to continue on to the Loire Valley by surface transport, as there's no air connection.)

International jet-setters will delight in the quiet informality at Tours airport—no bustling corps of porters nor noisy counters of duty-free shops and snack-bars as at big international airports. But taxi drivers are on hand to take you into town.

Airport information, tel. 54.19.46

BABY-SITTERS★ *(garde d'enfants)*. Most hotels will organize this but may do no more than send someone to "look in" periodically. If you want somebody on hand throughout your absence, it's best to approach your room maid. There's no set rate, and you must settle on a sum agreeable to both, on an hourly basis.

Can you get me/us a baby-sitter for tonight?	**Pouvez-vous me/nous trouver une garde d'enfants pour ce soir?**

BICYCLE★ **and MOPED HIRE** *(location de bicyclettes/vélomoteurs)*. Cycling being a highly popular sport in France, it's possible to hire bicycles in most of the Loire Valley towns. French National Railways *(SNCF)* operate a cycle-hire service at Amboise, Blois, Tours and Orléans stations. Bicycles may be hired at one station and returned at another.

Mopeds (motorbikes), called *vélomoteurs* or *cyclomoteurs,* shouldn't be difficult to find either; enquire at local tourist offices.

I'd like to hire a bicycle.	**Je voudrais louer une bicyclette.**
for one day/a week	**pour une journée/une semaine**

107

CAMPING* *(camping)*. Camping in France is a highly organized industry. There are over 200 official sites in the Loire Valley alone, between Orléans and Angers. Most of them offer attractive locations and excellent facilities.

Officially approved sites are classified on an ascending scale from one to four stars, depending on their amenities. If you're planning to camp, you should obtain the invaluable booklet *Pays de Loire—camping/caravanning* from the French Tourist Office in your country (see TOURIST INFORMATION OFFICES). In season (June to September), it's wise to book in advance.

Authorities of smaller localities sometimes permit free camping (the sign reads *camping autorisé*) on open sites with no amenities. A *camping interdit* notice means it's forbidden, however attractive the site may be. If you prefer to go it alone and camp where your fancy takes you, make sure you first obtain the landowner's permission.

Have you room for a tent/a caravan?	**Avez-vous de la place pour une tente/une caravane?**
May we camp on your land, please?	**Pouvons-nous camper sur votre terrain?**

CAR HIRE* *(location de voitures)*. See also DRIVING. Car hire agencies in France mainly handle French-made vehicles. Some firms offer unlimited-mileage package deals as well as fly-drive facilities. French National Railways also has a *train + auto* hire service available at Orléans, Blois, Tours, Saumur and Angers stations. Your travel agent will advise.

To hire a car you must produce a valid driving licence (held for at least one year) and your passport. Some firms set a minimum age at 21, others 25. Holders of major credit cards are normally exempt from deposit payments.

I'd like to hire a car (tomorrow).	**Je voudrais louer une voiture (demain).**
for one day/a week	**pour une journée/une semaine**
Please include full insurance.	**Avec assurance tous risques, s'il vous plaît.**

CIGARETTES, CIGARS, TOBACCO* *(cigarettes; cigares; tabac)*. Tobacco is a state monopoly in France, and the best place to buy your "smoke" is at an official *débit de tabac* (licensed tobacconist's). There are plenty of these—cafés, bars and many news-stands—bearing the conspicuous sign *Bar-Tabac* or *Tabac-Journaux* and a double red cone.

A packet of ..., please.	**Un paquet de ..., s'il vous plaît.**
light/dark tobacco	**du tabac blond/brun**
filter-tipped/without filter	**avec/sans filtre**
A box of matches, please.	**Une boîte d'allumettes, s'il vous plaît.**

CLOTHING. The Loire Valley enjoys a generally mild year-round climate. In winter, however, warm but not heavy clothing is advisable. In spring, summer and autumn, take along a light raincoat just in case and a sweater or wrap for the evenings.

When visiting churches, sober clothing should be worn, though headscarves for women are no longer required.

| Will I need a jacket and tie? | **Dois-je porter un veston et une cravate?** |

COMMUNICATIONS

Post office *(poste)*. You can identify French post offices by a sign with a stylized blue bird and/or the words *Postes et Télécommunications* or P & T. In cities, the main post office is open from 8 a.m. to 5 p.m., Monday to Friday, and 8 a.m. to noon on Saturdays. In smaller towns the hours are from 8.30 a.m. to noon, and 2.30 to 5 or 6 p.m., Monday to Friday; 8 a.m. to noon on Saturdays.

In addition to normal mail service, you can make local or long-distance telephone calls, send telegrams and receive or send money at any time at the post office.

Note: You can also buy stamps at a tobacconist's.

Poste restante (general delivery). If you don't know ahead of time where you'll be staying, you can have your mail addressed to you c/o *poste restante* to any town. Towns with more than one post office keep mail at the main post office *(poste principale)*. You'll have to show your passport to retrieve mail.

Telegrams. All local post offices accept telegrams, domestic or overseas. You may also dictate a telegram over the telephone (dial 14).

Telephone *(téléphone)*. International or long-distance calls can be made from phone boxes, but if you need assistance in placing the call, go to the post office or ask at your hotel. If you want to make a transferred-charge (collect) call, ask for *un appel en PCV* (pronounced: pay-say-

C

vay). For a personal (person-to-person) call, specify *un appel avec préavis pour...* (naming the party you want to talk to).

Local calls can also be made from cafés, where you might have to buy a *jeton* (token) to put into the phone.

express (special delivery)	**exprès**
airmail	**par avion**
registered	**recommandé**

A stamp for this letter/ postcard, please.	**Un timbre pour cette lettre/ carte postale, s'il vous plaît.**
I want to send a telegram to...	**J'aimerais envoyer un télégramme à...**
Have you any mail for...?	**Avez-vous du courrier pour...?**
Can you get me this number in...?	**Pouvez-vous me donner ce numéro à...?**

COMPLAINTS. If you fail to obtain on-the-spot satisfaction in the case of a justifiable and serious complaint, you can refer the matter to the nearest police station *(commissariat de police)*. If they cannot help, apply to the regional administration offices *(préfecture* or *sous-préfecture)*, asking for the *service du tourisme*. As to poor-quality merchandise, reputable stores usually exchange goods within 10 days of purchase, if you have your receipt.

CONVERTER CHARTS. For fluid and distance measures, see p. 113. France uses the metric system.

Temperature

°C
°F

Length

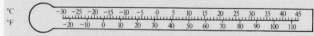

cm
inches
metres
ft./yd.

Weight

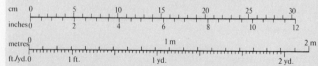

grams
oz.

110

CRIME and THEFT *(délit; vol)*. If you have items of real value, keep them in the hotel safe and obtain a receipt for them; it's a good idea to leave large amounts of money and even your passport there as well.

Another wise precaution is to keep any valuables out of sight, especially when you leave your car. Any loss or theft should be reported at once to the nearest *commissariat de police* or *gendarmerie* (see POLICE).

I want to report a theft.	**Je veux signaler un vol.**
My ticket/wallet/passport has been stolen.	**On a volé mon billet/portefeuille/ passeport.**

CUSTOMS *(douane)* **and ENTRY REGULATIONS.** See also DRIVING. Most visitors need only a valid passport—no visa—to enter France. British subjects can even enter on the simplified Visitor's Card. Though Europeans and North American residents are not subject to any health requirements, visitors from further afield may require a smallpox vaccination. Check with your travel agent before departure.

The following chart shows what main duty-free items you may take into France and, when returning home, into your own country (for passengers of 17 and older):

Into:	Cigarettes		Cigars		Tobacco	Spirits		Wine
France [1]	400		100		500 g.	1 l.		2 l.
[2]	300	or	75	or	400 g.	1½ l.	and	4 l.
[3]	200		50		250 g.	1 l.		2 l.
Canada	200	and	50	and	900 g.	1.1 l.	or	1.1 l.
Eire	300	or	75	or	400 g.	1½ l.	and	3 l.
U.K.	200	or	50	or	250 g.	1 l.	and	2 l.
U.S.A.	200	and	100	and	[4]	1 l.	or	1 l.

[1] Visitors arriving from outside Europe
[2] Visitors arriving from EEC countries with non duty-free items
[3] Visitors arriving from EEC countries with duty-free items and visitors from other European countries
[4] A reasonable quantity

Currency restrictions: There's no limit on the import of foreign currencies or traveller's cheques, but you may not leave the country with 111

C more than 5,000 French francs or the equivalent in foreign currency. If you plan to bring more than this sum in your own currency, you must establish a declaration on entry to enable you to re-export the same amount without trouble.

I've nothing to declare.	**Je n'ai rien à déclarer.**
It's for my own use.	**C'est pour mon usage personnel.**

D **DRIVING IN FRANCE.** To take a car into France, you'll need:
- a valid driving licence
- car registration papers
- insurance coverage (the most common formula is the Green Card)
- a national identity sticker
- a red warning triangle
- a set of spare bulbs

The Touring Club de France will advise members of affiliated organizations on itineraries, car repairs, etc. There are branch offices in:

Orléans, Maison du Tourisme, Place Albert-1er

Tours, 6, rue Emile-Zola

Driving regulations. The use of seat belts is obligatory. Driving with dipped headlights is required in built-up areas. All the basic rules for right-hand traffic apply: drive on the right, pass on the left, yield right of way to all vehicles coming from the right (even on roundabouts [traffic circles], unless otherwise indicated).

Speed limits in force are 60 kilometres per hour (37 m.p.h.) in towns and residential areas, 90 k.p.h. (56 m.p.h.) on open roads and 130 k.p.h. (81 m.p.h.) on motorways (expressways). Respect these limits strictly; controls are getting tighter.

The French style of driving can be terrifying if you're not used to it, with plenty of speed and daring overtaking. Stick to your own pace and keep a safe distance between yourself and the vehicle in front.

Road conditions. French roads are designated by an A, standing for *autoroute* (motorway); an N for national highways; a D for *départementale*, or regional roads; and a V for local roads *(chemins vicinaux)*. In recent years, road surfaces have been greatly improved. The *nationales*, or major highways, are good on the whole but often not as wide as they could be, especially at the time when most French people go on holiday: the 1st and 15th of July, the 1st and 15th of August and the 1st of September.

The motorways are excellent and owned by public companies which charge tolls according to vehicle size and distance travelled. All amenities (restaurants, toilets, service stations, etc.) are available, plus orange S.O.S. telephones every 2 kilometres.

Many tourists like to travel on secondary roads at a more leisurely pace with better views. Sometimes you'll find alternative routes *(itinéraires bis)* sign-posted along the way by emerald-green arrows.

Parking. In town centres, most street parking is metered. The blue zones require the *disque de stationnement* or parking clock (obtainable from petrol stations or stationers), which you set to show when you arrived and when you must leave. Some streets have alternate parking on either side of the street according to which part of the month it is (the dates are marked on the signs). Fines for parking violations can be heavy, and in serious cases your car may be towed away or have a "Denver boot" attached (a metal tire lock that cannot be released until you pay up at the local *commissariat,* or police station).

Breakdowns. Towing and on-the-spot repairs can be made by local garages, and spare parts are readily available for European cars. It's wise to take out some form of internationally valid breakdown insurance before leaving home, and always ask for an estimate *before* undertaking repairs. There's a TVA charge on top of repairs.

Traffic police. The *Garde Mobile* patrols the roads and motorways in cars or on powerful motorcycles. Always in pairs, they are courteous and helpful but extremely severe on lawbreakers and have authority to fine offenders on the spot.

Fuel and oil *(essence; huile).* Fuel is available in *super* and *normale.* Prices are regularly on the increase, making petrol in France one of Europe's most expensive. Service-station attendants are left as a rule a small tip.

Fluid measures

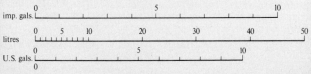

Distance

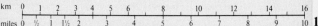

D **Road signs.** Most road signs are the standard pictographs used throughout Europe, but you may encounter these written signs as well:

Accotements non stabilisés	Soft shoulders
Chaussée déformée	Bad road surface
Déviation	Diversion (detour)
Douane	Customs
Gravillons	Loose gravel
Impasse	Cul-de-sac (dead-end)
Péage	Toll
Priorité à droite	Yield to traffic from right
Ralentir	Slow
Sauf riverains	Entry prohibited except for inhabitants of street
Sens unique	One-way street
Serrez à droite/gauche	Keep right/left
Sortie de camions	Lorry (truck) exit
Stationnement interdit	No parking
Véhicules lents	Slow vehicles

(international) driving licence	**permis de conduire (international)**
car registration papers	**carte grise**
Are we on the right road for...?	**Sommes-nous sur la route de...?**
Full tank, please.	**Le plein, s'il vous plaît.**
regular/super	**normale/super**
Check the oil/tires/battery.	**Veuillez contrôler l'huile/les pneus/la batterie.**
I've had a breakdown.	**Ma voiture est en panne.**
There's been an accident.	**Il y a eu un accident.**

E **ELECTRIC CURRENT.** 220-volt, 50-cycle A.C. is now almost universal, though 110 volts may still be encountered. British and American visitors using electric appliances should remember to buy a Continental adaptor plug before leaving home. They can also be bought in some electric supply shops *(magasins d'électricité)* or *drogueries*.

What's the voltage—110 or 220?	**Quel est le voltage – cent dix ou deux cent vingt?**
an adaptor plug/a battery	**une prise de raccordement/une pile**

EMBASSIES and CONSULATES. Embassies and consulates are listed in the telephone books under "Ambassades" and "Consulats". There are no British, Commonwealth or U.S. consulates in the Loire Valley. In case of need (loss of passport, trouble with the police or serious accident), contact your embassy or consulate in Paris.

Canada	Consulate: 4, rue Ventadour, 75001 Paris; tel. 296.87.19. Off-hour emergencies (embassy), tel. 225.99.55
Eire	Embassy: 12, avenue Foch (visitors' entrance from 4, rue Rude), 75016 Paris; tel. 500.20.87
Great Britain	Consulate: 105–109, rue du Faubourg Saint-Honoré, 75008 Paris; tel. 266.91.42
U.S.A.	Embassy and consulate: 4, avenue Gabriel, 75008 Paris; tel. 296.12.02

Where's the embassy/consulate?	**Où se trouve l'ambassade/le consulat?**
I'd like to phone the... embassy.	**Je voudrais téléphoner à l'ambassade...**
American/British	**américaine/britannique**
Canadian/Irish	**canadienne/irlandaise**

EMERGENCIES. See also under EMBASSIES AND CONSULATES, HEALTH AND MEDICAL CARE, etc., according to the type of emergency.

The emergency numbers below cover the whole country. If you don't speak French, try English or ask the first person you see to help you call.

Police *(Police-Secours)*	17
Fire, ambulance *(pompiers)*	18

These words are handy to know in difficult situations:

Fire	**Au feu**
Help	**Au secours**
Police	**Police**
Stop	**Arrêtez**
Can you help me?	**Pouvez-vous m'aider?**
Call a doctor/an ambulance, quickly!	**Appelez d'urgence un médecin/une ambulance!**

GUIDES* and INTERPRETERS *(guide; interprète)*. Local *syndicats d'initiative* (see TOURIST INFORMATION OFFICES) can supply or direct you to qualified official guides and interpreters if you want a personally

G conducted tour or any linguistic assistance. Guides engaged for a whole day should be offered lunch.

Bus companies also offer many guided tours. It's customary to tip the guide.

We'd like an English-speaking guide.	**Nous aimerions un guide parlant anglais.**
I need an English interpreter.	**J'ai besoin d'un interprète anglais.**

H **HAIRDRESSERS* and BARBERS** *(coiffeur)*. Prices vary widely according to the class of establishment, but rates are usually displayed in the window in any case. Most establishments include *service* in the price, but it's customary to give a little something to the person who washes your hair, and a tip to the stylist.

I'd like...	**Je voudrais...**
a haircut	**une coupe de cheveux**
a shampoo and set	**un shampooing et mise en plis**
a blow-dry	**un brushing**
the colour chart	**le nuancier**
a colour rinse/a hair-dye	**un rinçage/une teinture**
Don't cut it too short (here).	**Pas trop court (ici), s'il vous plaît.**
A little more off (here).	**Un peu plus court (ici).**

HEALTH and MEDICAL CARE. See also EMERGENCIES. To be at ease, make sure your health insurance policy covers any illness or accident while on holiday. If not, ask your insurance representative, automobile association or travel agent for details of special travel insurance.

Visitors from EEC countries with corresponding health insurance facilities are entitled to medical and hospital treatment under the French social security system. Before leaving home, make sure you find out about the appropriate form(s) required to obtain this benefit in case of need. Doctors who belong to the French social security system *(médecins conventionnés)* charge the minimum.

The "tourist's complaint" that hits many travellers is not due to drinking tap water, which is safe in towns all over France. Fatigue, too much sun, change of diet and over-indulgence are the main causes of most minor complaints. Be careful about over-eating and, especially, drinking. French mineral water is a good thirst quencher and helps to digest meals. Serious gastro-intestinal problems lasting more than a day
or two should be looked after by a doctor.

Chemists or **drugstores** are easily recognized by a green cross. The personnel is helpful in dealing with minor ailments or in finding a nurse *(infirmière)* if you need injections or other special care.

Where's the nearest (all-night) chemist?	**Où se trouve la pharmacie (de garde) la plus proche?**
I need a doctor/dentist.	**Il me faut un médecin/dentiste.**
I've a pain here.	**J'ai mal ici.**
stomach ache	**mal à l'estomac**
headache	**mal à la tête**
fever	**de la fièvre**

HITCH-HIKING *(auto-stop)*. This is permitted everywhere except on motorways. If you do hitch-hike, it's always wiser to go in pairs.

Can you give me/us a lift to...?	**Pouvez-vous m'emmener/nous emmener à...?**

LANGUAGE. In the Loire Valley, and especially in Touraine, you'll be treated to the clearest, purest French spoken in France. There are no local dialects.

The Berlitz phrase book FRENCH FOR TRAVELLERS covers almost all situations you're likely to encounter in your travels in France. If further help is required, the Berlitz French-English/English-French pocket dictionary contains the basic vocabulary a tourist will need, plus a menu-reader supplement.

Good morning/Good afternoon	**Bonjour**
Good afternoon/Good evening	**Bonsoir**
Please	**S'il vous plaît**
Thank you	**Merci**
You're welcome	**Je vous en prie**
Goodbye	**Au revoir**

LAUNDRY and DRY-CLEANING *(blanchisserie; nettoyage à sec)*. If your hotel will not take care of laundry or cleaning, you can have clothes cleaned quickly and cheaply in chain dry-cleaners (not recommended, however, for fragile fabrics or difficult spots). Better care takes longer and is more expensive; prices vary according to fabric and cut.

When will it be ready?	**Quand est-ce que ce sera prêt?**
I must have it tomorrow morning.	**Il me le faut pour demain matin.**

L **LOST PROPERTY** *(objets trouvés)*. If loss or suspected theft occurs in your hotel, check first at the desk. They may suggest you report the loss to the local police station *(commissariat de police* or *gendarmerie)*. Restaurant and café personnel are quite honest about returning objects left behind; they turn valuables over to the police.

I've lost my wallet/ handbag/passport.	**J'ai perdu mon portefeuille/ sac à main/passeport.**

M **MAPS.** Various detailed topographical and road maps exist for motorists and hikers. Particularly useful is Michelin's No. 64. Simplified city maps are generally included in the range of free-of-charge tourist brochures to be found at travel agencies, tourist offices and hotels.

The maps in this book were prepared by Falk-Verlag, Hamburg, who also publish a map of France.

Do you have a map of the city/the region?	**Avez-vous un plan de la ville/ une carte de la région?**

MEETING PEOPLE. Loire Valley people, whether town- or country-dwellers, had, and still have, a special reputation in France for good-naturedness and courtesy, as you'll certainly find out for yourself. The local people do not, however—like most French—have much taste for foreign languages; a smattering of French, or at least an attempt to say the odd word, is therefore appreciated.

Don't be surprised if someone says *bonsoir* (good evening) to you at 9 in the morning. It's the accepted daily greeting around these parts. Wherever you find yourself, a simple *bonjour* (good day), a smile, a *s'il vous plaît* (please) or a *merci* (thanks) will go a long way.

In restaurants and cafés, *garçon* is the customary way to call a waiter *(mademoiselle* for a waitress), or you can simply say *s'il vous plaît.* The *maître d'hôtel* (headwaiter) and *sommelier* (wine steward) are addressed as *monsieur.*

If you stop a policeman or passerby to ask for directions, start with *excusez-moi, Monsieur/Madame.*

French people kiss or shake hands when greeting each other or saying goodbye. When you're introduced to someone or meeting a friend you're expected to shake hands at least. Close friends are kissed on both cheeks.

Good day!	**Bonjour!**
I'm glad to meet you.	**Enchanté.**
How are you?	**Comment allez-vous?**

118

MONEY MATTERS

Currency. The French *franc* (abbreviated *F* or *FF*) is divided into 100 *centimes (cts)*.

Coins: 5, 10, 20, 50 cts; 1, 2, 5, 10 F.

Banknotes: 10, 20, 50, 100, 200, 500 F.

For currency restrictions, see CUSTOMS AND ENTRY REGULATIONS.

Banks and currency exchange. Though hours can vary, French banks are generally open from 8.30 a.m. to noon and from 2 to 5.30 p.m., Monday to Friday. In large towns like Angers, Blois, Orléans, Saumur and Tours, some are open on Saturdays. The banks that open on Saturday are closed on Monday. All banks close on certain holidays (see PUBLIC HOLIDAYS).

If you need to change money outside normal banking hours, your hotel will usually come to the rescue, though you'll get a less favourable rate of exchange. The same applies to foreign currency or traveller's cheques changed in stores, boutiques or restaurants. Most local tourist offices will change money outside banking hours at the official bank rate. Take your passport along when you go to change money or traveller's cheques.

Credit cards may be used in an increasing number of hotels, restaurants, shops, etc. Signs are posted indicating which cards are accepted.

Traveller's cheques are widely accepted throughout France, but outside the towns, it's preferable to have some ready cash with you.

Be sure to keep your purchaser's receipt and a listing by serial number of the cheques separately from the cheques themselves, as these will be necessary to get a refund in case of loss or theft.

Eurocheques are accepted by a wide range of businesses.

Sales tax. Called *TVA*, the sales (value added) tax of 17.6% is imposed on almost all goods and services. In hotels and restaurants, this is accompanied by a service charge (see TIPPING).

Visitors returning home to a non-EEC country can avoid paying the *TVA* on larger purchases. You must fill out a form, give a copy to the customs when leaving France and will later receive your refund at home.

Where's the nearest bank/currency exchange office?	**Où se trouve la banque/le bureau de change la/le plus proche?**
I want to change some pounds/dollars.	**Je voudrais changer des livres sterling/dollars.**
Do you accept traveller's cheques/this credit card?	**Acceptez-vous les chèques de voyage/cette carte de crédit?**

N **NEWSPAPERS and MAGAZINES** *(journal; revue)*. During the tourist season, you can be certain of getting major British and Continental newspapers and magazines on publication day or the following morning, including the Paris-based *International Herald Tribune*.

Have you any English-language newspapers?	**Avez-vous des journaux en anglais?**

P **PHOTOGRAPHY.** Amateur photography is always permitted outside the châteaux, but inside them only in the state-owned ones, and at an extra charge.

All popular film makes and sizes are available; rapid development is possible, though sometimes expensive.

Some airport security machines use X-rays, which can ruin your film. Ask that it be checked separately, or enclose it in a film-shield.

I'd like a film for this camera.	**J'aimerais un film pour cet appareil.**
a black-and-white film	**un film noir et blanc**
a film for colour prints	**un film couleurs**
a colour-slide film	**un film pour diapositives**
35–mm film	**un film de trente-cinq millimètre**
super 8	**un film super-huit**
How long will it take to develop this film?	**Combien de temps faut-il pour développer ce film?**
May I take a picture?	**Puis-je prendre une photo?**

POLICE. In cities and larger towns you'll see the blue-uniformed *police municipale;* they are the local police force who keep order, investigate crime and direct traffic. Outside of the main towns are the *gendarmes*—they wear blue trousers and black jackets with white belts and are also responsible for traffic and crime investigation. The C.R.S. police *(Compagnies Républicaines de Sécurité)* are a national security force responsible to the Ministry of the Interior and are called in for emergencies and special occasions. The *Garde Mobile,* or *Police de la Route,* patrol the roads.

In case of need, dial 17 anywhere in France for police help.

Where's the nearest police station?	**Où est le poste de police le plus proche?**

PUBLIC HOLIDAYS *(jour férié)*

January 1	*Jour de l'An*	New Year's Day
May 1	*Fête du Travail*	Labour Day
July 14	*Fête Nationale*	Bastille Day
August 15	*Assomption*	Assumption
November 1	*Toussaint*	All Saints' Day
November 11	*Armistice*	Armistice Day
December 25	*Noël*	Christmas Day
Movable dates:	*Lundi de Pâques*	Easter Monday
	Ascension	Ascension
	Lundi de Pentecôte	Whit Monday

These are the national French holidays. See page 77 for details of local celebrations and events.

Are you open tomorrow?	**Etes-vous ouvert demain?**

RADIO and TV *(radio; télévision)*. There are three TV channels in France, all in colour. Programmes begin rather late in the day. Some hotels have television in the lounges, many in the top categories have sets in the rooms.

BBC programmes can be heard on short or medium-wave radios. In summer the French radio broadcasts news and information in English.

RELIGIOUS SERVICES *(office religieux)*. The majority religion of France is Roman Catholic. Times of mass are always posted at church entrances. You'll also find these times on roadside signboards as you drive into smaller towns and villages.

Protestant (Reformed) services *(culte protestant)* are held at Orléans, Blois, Tours, Saumur and Angers. There are no English-language services.

Jewish services *(culte israélite)* are conducted at Orléans and Tours.

Hotel receptionists, policemen and tourist office personnel can supply further information.

Where is the Protestant church/ synagogue?	**Où se trouve l'église protestante/ la synagogue?**
What time is mass/the service?	**A quelle heure est la messe/ le culte?**

TIME DIFFERENCES. The following chart shows the time differences between France and various cities in winter. In summer, French clocks are put forward one hour.

Los Angeles	Chicago	New York	London	**France**
3 a.m.	5 a.m.	6 a.m.	11 a.m.	**noon**

What time is it?   **Quelle heure est-il?**

TIPPING. A 10 to 15% service charge is generally included automatically in hotel and restaurant bills. Rounding off the overall bill helps round off friendships with waiters, too. Taxi drivers should get 10–15%, as should women's hairdressers and barbers. See the chart below for further guidelines.

Porter, per bag	1– 3 F
Hotel maid, per week	10–15 F
Bellboy, errand	1– 2 F
Lavatory attendant	1– 1.50 F
Filling station attendant	1– 3 F
Guide, half day	10–15 F
Cinema usher	1– 2 F

TOILETS. Clean public conveniences are still not all that common in France, and the stand-up toilet facilities can be rather harrowing. If there is no light-switch, the light will usually go on when you lock the door. Three-star WCs do exist, mostly in better hotels and restaurants.

Café facilities are generally free, but you should order at least a coffee if you use the toilet. A saucer with small change on it means that a tip is expected. The women's toilets may be marked *Dames;* the men's either *Messieurs* or *Hommes.*

Where are the toilets, please?   **Où sont les toilettes, s'il vous plaît?**

TOURIST INFORMATION OFFICES *(office du tourisme).* French national tourist offices can help you plan your holiday and will supply you with a wide range of colourful, informative brochures and maps.

Some addresses:

Canada	1840 Ouest, rue Sherbrooke, Montreal H3H 1E4, P.Q.; tel. (514) 931-3855
	372 Bay Street, Suite 610, Toronto, Ont. M5H 2W9; tel. (416) 361-1605
Great Britain	178, Piccadilly, London W1V 0AL; tel. (01) 491-7622
U.S.A.	645 N. Michigan Avenue, Suite 430, Chicago, IL 60611; tel. (312) 337-6301
	9401 Wilshire Boulevard, Room 840, Beverly Hills, CA 90212; tel. (213) 271-6665
	610 Fifth Avenue, New York, NY 10020; tel. (212) 757-1125
	Post Street, Suite 601, San Francisco, CA 94108; tel. (415) 982-7272

On the spot:

Amboise	Syndicat d'Initiative, Mail du Général de Gaulle; tel. (47) 59.07.28
Angers	Office du Tourisme, 71, rue Plantagenêt, tel. (41) 88.69.93
Blois	Office du Tourisme, Pavillon Anne de Bretagne, 3, avenue Jean Laigret; tel. (54) 74.06.49/78.23.21
Orléans	Office du Tourisme, Place Albert-1er; tel. (38) 53.05.95
Saumur	Syndicat d'Initiative, 25, rue Beaurepaire; tel. (41) 51.03.06
Tours	Office du Tourisme, Place de la Gare; tel. (47) 05.58.08

Local tourist information offices *(syndicat d'initiative)* are invaluable sources of information (from maps to hotel lists and other miscellaneous items) in all French towns. They are usually found near the town's centre and often have a branch at the railway station. Opening hours vary, but the general rule is 8.30 or 9 a.m. to noon and from 2 to 6 or 7 p.m., every day except Sunday.

Where's the tourist office, please?	**Où est le syndicat d'initiative, s'il vous plaît?**

TRANSPORT. See also Car Hire.

Buses* *(autobus/autocar)*. Bus terminals are invariably close to the railway station, and you'll find route and other information there. Some

T of the transport companies also organize special coach tours of local châteaux, as do the French National Railways.

Taxis. You'll find no lack of taxi services throughout the region. In the larger towns, there are stands at the stations as well as in the centre. Taxis can be called by telephone everywhere, including smaller localities. Local tourist brochures give taxi phone numbers.

Rates can vary from place to place. They're usually higher in smaller towns, where runs are shorter, and from all stations where a pick-up and luggage rate (per piece) are charged. If you have a good distance to go, ask the fare beforehand.

Trains. SNCF—Société Nationale des Chemins de Fer Français or the French National Railways—run fast, clean and efficient trains. There are excellent regular services from Paris-Montparnasse to Angers, and from Paris-Austerlitz to Blois, Orléans and Tours. Orléans is a stone's throw away by train, and a direct express from Paris takes you to Tours in just an hour and a half, a distance of 150 miles. High-speed trains are in service most of the time.

Local rail connections are equally good and backed up by a network of SNCF-operated bus and coach services.

SNCF offer various categories of ticket, like *Billet Touristique, Billet de Groupes, Billet de Famille, France-Vacances*, etc. Enquire at the nearest *syndicat d'initiative* or railway information counter. *Eurailpasses* and *Inter-Rail Cards* (see pp. 102–103) are valid in France.

When's the next bus/train to...?	**Quand part le prochain bus/ train pour...?**
When's the best train to...?	**A quelle heure part le meilleur train pour...?**
single (one-way)	**aller simple**
return (round-trip)	**aller et retour**
first/second class	**première/deuxième classe**
I'd like to make seat reservations.	**J'aimerais réserver des places.**
Where can I get a taxi?	**Où puis-je trouver un taxi?**

W **WATER.** Tap water is safe throughout the country, except when marked *eau non potable* (not safe for drinking). A wide variety of mineral water can be found on sale everywhere.

a bottle of mineral water carbonated/non-carbonated	**une bouteille d'eau minérale gazeuse/non gazeuse**
Is this drinking water?	**Est-ce de l'eau potable?**

SOME USEFUL EXPRESSIONS

yes/no	oui/non
please/thank you	s'il vous plaît/merci
excuse me	excusez-moi
you're welcome	je vous en prie
where/when/how	où/quand/comment
how long/how far	combien de temps/à quelle distance
yesterday/today/tomorrow	hier/aujourd'hui/demain
day/week/month/year	jour/semaine/mois/année
left/right	gauche/droite
up/down	en haut/en bas
good/bad	bon/mauvais
big/small	grand/petit
cheap/expensive	bon marché/cher
hot/cold	chaud/froid
old/new	vieux/neuf
open/closed	ouvert/fermé
here/there	ici/là
free (vacant)/occupied	libre/occupé
early/late	tôt/tard
easy/difficult	facile/difficile
Does anyone here speak English?	Y a-t-il quelqu'un ici qui parle anglais?
What does this mean?	Que signifie ceci?
I don't understand.	Je ne comprends pas.
Please write it down.	Ecrivez-le-moi, s'il vous plaît.
Is there an admission charge?	Faut-il payer pour entrer?
Waiter/Waitress!	Garçon/Mademoiselle!
I'd like...	J'aimerais...
How much is that?	C'est combien?
Have you something less expensive?	Avez-vous quelque chose de moins cher?
What time is it?	Quelle heure est-il?
Help me please.	Aidez-moi, s'il vous plaît.

Index

An asterisk (*) next to a page number indicates a map reference. The individual châteaux are grouped alphabetically under the heading of Châteaux.

4/82 SUD